C000179059

TRADITIONAL
Folk Art

Left to right: Oval and Heart-Shaped Belt Buckles *(pages 34 and 35)*, Round Marbled Brooch *(page 36)*, Heart-Shaped Brooch *(page 37)*, Roses and Berries Bracelet *(page 39)*, Daisy Bracelet *(page 38)*.

Ceramic Decorative Pots *(page 46)*, Metal Creamer *(page 48)*.

TRADITIONAL
Folk Art

A COMPLETE GUIDE TO PAINTING FOLK ART

Janet Klepatzki

Oval Timber Box *(page 43)*, Ceramic Daisy Duck *(page 41)*.

BLITZ EDITIONS

Foreword

Folk art is a method of painting which can be learnt by anyone. All you need is the desire to be creative and a willingness to spend the time learning. It is a learning process that will create constant excitement whenever you pick up a paint brush. You can achieve whatever level of painting that pleases you and makes you happy.

Most folk artists are not born with a God given artistic ability but learn their craft from someone who is willing to teach them; therefore, they feel a responsibility to share that knowledge with someone else. Everything can be made a little more beautiful by the addition of a personal touch of colour — whether in a flower, a scroll or just decorating brush strokes.

The desire to share our folk art knowledge puts us in contact with other people and, because folk art is not something that is exclusive to any particular people or country, the world becomes smaller and our world of friends enlarges. My painting friends throughout several countries are, I feel, an extension of my family and I am grateful that I have had the opportunity for our paths to cross.

Within the following pages you will find a thorough and complete, instructional book of folk art. It is so complete that it should give you many hours of enjoyment of the wonderful adventure that is folk art, and open up the exciting world of painting for you.

May all your painting hours be happy hours!

Bette Byrd, M.D.A.
Atlanta, Georgia, U.S.A.

Contents

Foreword   4
Colour Worksheets and Photographs 1–16
Author's Note   17
Folk Art Alphabet   18

Part One:
An Introduction to Folk Art   19
1 History of Folk Art   20
2 Getting Started: The Materials   21
3 Basic Brushstrokes   23
4 Preparation of Surfaces   26
5 Wood Staining and Antiquing   28
6 Hints for Painting the Design   30

Part Two:
Projects to Paint   33
Heart-Shaped Belt Buckle   34
Oval Belt Buckle   35
Round Marbled Brooch   36
Heart-Shaped Brooch   37
Daisy Bracelet   38
Roses and Berries Bracelet   39
Ceramic Daisy Duck   41
Oval Timber Box   43
Ceramic Decorative Pots   46
Metal Creamer   48
Small Wooden Jar   50
Wooden Counter Bell   51
Austrian Wooden Plate   53

Wooden Egg   56
Timber Key Holder   58
Small Wooden Pan   60
Old Parlour Heater   62
Old Dairy Bucket   64
Antiqued Coal-Scuttle   66
Colonial Kettle with Australian
    Bouquet   68
Small Picture Frame   70
Oval Picture Frame   72
Metal Lunch Box   74
Rose-covered Jewellery Box   76
Tulip-Garland Parlour Clock   78
Breakfast Tray   80
Timber Welcome Sign   82
Timber Coat Rack   84
Wooden Spoon Holder   86
Stained Timber Stool   88
Painter's Case   91
Wooden Box with
    Bavarian Couple   96
Wooden Clogs   98
Seaman's Uniform Trunk   101
Cow Bell   104
Antiqued Bavarian Wall Clock   106
Our House Sign   108

Index   110
Acknowledgments   112

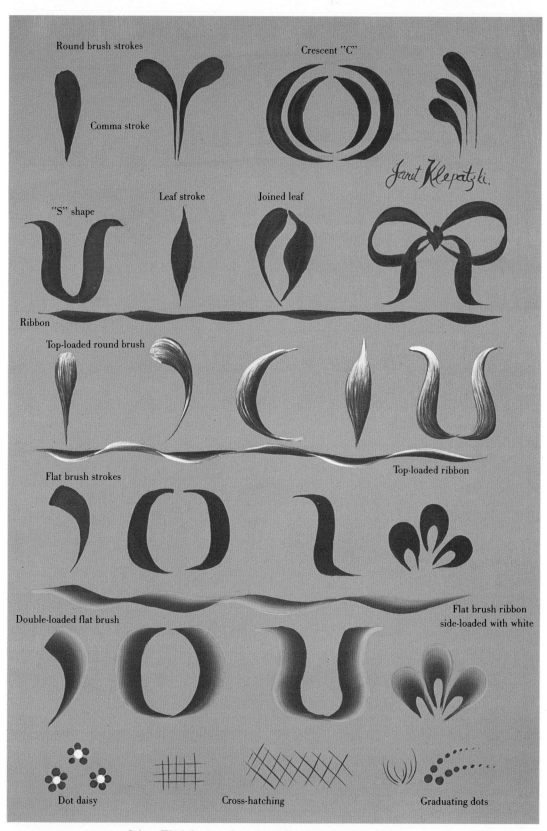

Round brush strokes

Comma stroke

Crescent "C"

Jaret Klepatski.

"S" shape

Leaf stroke

Joined leaf

Ribbon

Top-loaded round brush

Top-loaded ribbon

Flat brush strokes

Double-loaded flat brush

Flat brush ribbon
side-loaded with white

Dot daisy

Cross-hatching

Graduating dots

Colour Worksheet — Round and Flat Brushstrokes, Commas.

6

Colour Worksheet — Fruit, Flower and Scene Details.

Comma strokes border

Closed Bauernmalerei Rose

Daisy

Flat brush rose

Rosebuds trim

Lace border (use stylus)

Hindeloopen flower

White daisy flower

Open rose

Border trim
(leaf and dot daisy)

Colour Worksheet — Roses, Daisies, Hindeloopen Flower.

8

Rope trim (Buttercrunch)

Sailing ship (Honeycomb)

Trim

Foreshore (Shamrock)

Bavarian scene

Bavarian couple

Sponge marbling

Colour Worksheet — Ship, Bavarian Couple and Scene, Sponge Marbling.

Colour Worksheet — Rose, Poppy, Tulip, Scroll Border.

Wooden Counter Bell *(page 51)*, Small Wooden Jar *(page 50)*, Austrian Wooden Plate *(page 53)*, Wooden Egg *(page 56)*.

Timber Key Holder *(page 58)*.

Small Wooden Pan *(page 60)*, Old Parlour Heater *(page 62)*.

Old Dairy Bucket *(page 64)*.

Colonial Kettle with Australian Bouquet *(page 68)*.   Antiqued Coal-Scuttle *(page 66)*.

Seaman's Uniform Trunk *(page 101)*.

Metal Lunch Box *(page 74)*, Small Picture Frame *(page 70)*, Oval Picture Frame *(page 72)*.

Breakfast Tray *(page 80)*, Rose-covered Jewellery Box *(page 76)*, Tulip–Garland Parlour Clock *(page 78)*.

Timber Welcome Sign *(page 82).*

Timber Coat Rack *(page 84),* Wooden Spoon Holder *(page 86).*

Stained Timber Stool *(page 88)*.

Antiqued Bavarian Wall Clock *(page 106)*.

Left to right: Cow Bell *(page 104)*, Wooden Box with Bavarian Couple *(page 96)*, Painter's Case *(page 91)*, Wooden Clogs *(page 98)*.

Our House Sign *(page 108)*.

Author's Note

I began painting with oils and watercolours in my late teens and studied under a wonderful teacher, who gave me a good grounding in design and colour mixing, but it wasn't until 1982, when travelling through my husband's homeland, Bavaria, that folk art had an impact on my life. There amid the landscapes, villages and towns of this beautiful area of Germany, folk art is everywhere – decorating the walls of houses and churches, on furniture in public places and homes, and in the museums. It inspired me to make folk art a part of my own work. I now have a studio in my home town of Camden, NSW, where I teach folk artists of the future.

I have written this book to share with you my interpretation of traditional folk art. The brushstrokes and designs have European origins, although there is also a bouquet of Australian flowers for you to paint. As well, there are several examples of the flat brush technique, which is now predominant in North American folk art. Painting with a flat brush blends the colours to show their value from light to dark, giving a degree of realism.

Perhaps the most important thing I should tell you here is that folk art is the 'Make Believe' realm of the art world, so you can relax while you paint, with no need to remember the strict guidelines of perspective and realism. Early folk artists concerned themselves only with decoration and colour, and painted a design that made them happy.

Before you start to paint, refer to the first sections of this book, covering materials, brushstrokes, surface preparations, staining and antiquing, pattern sizing and transfer, and design.

Now choose the project you wish to paint. Patterns vary in level from those for the beginner to those for the experienced painter, so choose one that you feel confident with. Beginner level projects include Belt Buckles, the Ceramic Daisy Duck, the Small Wooden Pan and the Welcome Sign.

Refer to the colour worksheets at the front of this book (pages 6 to 10) for the basic brushstrokes used in folk art. Here you will also find colour photographs of all the items to be painted. Then refer to the pattern and the detailed text instructions given for each project. Here you will find what paints to use from basecoat to highlights, what brushes to use, how to apply the paint and all the detail you need to create your own folk art pieces.

I have used FolkArt™ Acrylic Color paints throughout this book but you may use whichever brand you prefer.

I hope you will enjoy the wonderful, creative pastime of folk art as much as I do.

Janet Klepatzki

Dedication

To my Father and Mother, for their patience and guidance in bringing up a creative and inquisitive child.

An alphabet to follow when signing and dating your work

PART ONE
AN INTRODUCTION TO FOLK ART

1 History of Folk Art

'Folk art' is a modern term for the very old, traditional, cottage art. It was developed by farmers, carpenters and cabinetmakers in Europe from about the sixteenth century. During the long winter months they spent their time repairing tools and making simple pieces of furniture such as tables, cradles, boxes and benches, which they decorated with very simple paintwork. Pigment for the paint was found in their surroundings: black soot from the fire, white from lime, and green, blue and yellow from flowers and other parts of plants.

Folk artists generally had no formal training, and their only source of inspiration apart from the land around them, was the church and its ornate decorations. Religious symbols such as the heart, for love, and the tree, a sign of the earth, became incorporated in their more usual floral designs.

The folk artists could not afford the fine timbers and expensive inlays of the nobility and rich merchants, but they began to copy them using stencils and glazes to achieve the inlaid effect. Gradually over the centuries, this cottage-based tradition produced many beautiful works of art while still retaining its simplicity of design.

The early wooden pieces were only stained, as woodworm was prevalent in Europe and in many areas it was illegal to cover an item of furniture with coloured paint in case it hid the pest's holes.

The covering of woodwork with a full coat of coloured paint and heavy, colourful designs appeared in the first half of the eighteenth century. With the influence of the rococo style, colours became bright and clear, and flowers in art and crafts became more realistic.

During the period when the Biedermeier style was influential (about 1820–1850), the look of marble was a popular finish on the surface of wooden pieces. A gentle bow began to replace the more severe vase or basket in which floral bouquets were set. By the end of the nineteenth century painted furniture had become highly fashionable, and the beautiful old traditions were destined to continue with decorative painters who mastered the skills of past generations and created wonderful pieces for future generations to enjoy.

Modern folk art stems from each artist's interpretation of the basic brushstrokes that artists of earlier centuries were using. My instructions for brushstrokes may vary from the early traditional style but as individuals we must try to create our own style while retaining traditional techniques.

The designs featured have come from different areas of Europe, each country having its own unique style. With my style of folk art I want to interpret what I see around me and try to feel as those farmers and cabinetmakers did centuries ago.

2 Getting Started: The Materials

Early painters had to improvise and make their own brushes, paints and stains. Now, with modern technology, all we need is available from a local craft or art supply shop.

Brushes

I always recommend good-quality synthetic brushes for applying acrylic paints, because the paint is fast-drying and will not be absorbed as quickly into a synthetic fibre. If using natural hair or sable brushes, take extra care in cleaning.

A small collection of brushes:
No. 4 or 5 round brush, for most general painting.
No. 2 liner brush, for fine lines and detail.
No. 6 to 10 flat or shader brush, for flat brushwork.
Stipple brush (scruffy brush) for trees and bushes.
Large acrylic bristle brush (or house-painting brush) for basecoating large pieces.
As you gain experience you will no doubt collect many more brushes.
CARE OF BRUSHES After painting, wash the brush in cold water to remove most of the acrylic paint. Using normal household soap, gently roll the brush into the soap so that the excess paint dissolves, then rinse with cold water, and repeat the process. When the brush is clean, coat the fibres with a thin covering of soap and gently shape them into a fine point. The soap dries like a setting agent and protects the fibres, keeping them together in a fine point. Never leave a brush in the water jar or resting on its fibres. Store the brush upright in a brush container. Before you recommence painting, rinse the brush in cold water to remove the soap.

If paint builds up in the brush and the fibres do not return to a fine point suitable for painting, try a good commercial brand of brush cleaner. If that doesn't work, it's time to buy a new brush.

Paints

Water-based acrylic paints have a consistency that is just right for folk art and there is a wide range of colours to choose from. I have used FolkArt™ paints but you may use whichever acrylic folk art paints you prefer.

Medium

A medium (also known as Extender, Retarder, Acryl-blend) is added to the acrylic paint to slow the drying time. It is essential for flat brushwork and blending colours. (Adding water to the paint will dilute the colour and speed up the drying.) I have used FolkArt™ Extender.

Varnish

FolkArt™ Satin Finish Water Base Varnish is the one I use to seal and protect my painting when it is finished. FolkArt™ Hi-Shine Brilliant Glaze is used to varnish jewellery. There are others available.

A good sealer for your prepared surface before painting is 1 part water added to 1 part Satin Finish Water Base Varnish. Store in a sealed container. It can be used when referred to in the instruction 'Apply a thin coat of Satin Finish Water Base Varnish'.

Basic Equipment

PALETTE You can use a white porcelain tile or a large dinner plate, or commercial palette paper which can be re-used.
WATER JAR Always have two jars of water when painting, the second one for that extra rinse.
WHITE CHALK To freehand the pattern onto your piece.
TRANSFER PAPER Commercial transfer paper is specially made for folk art. There is a wide range of colours. Choose a dark colour for transferring a pattern onto a light background and a light colour for a dark background.
STYLUS This simple tool helps to transfer the pattern when using transfer paper and is useful for painting fine dots.
ERASER Most brands of erasers are suitable for removing transfer paper lines.
FINE WET AND DRY SANDPAPER Keep a few sheets of sandpaper (40-1200 grit) on hand.
TACK CLOTH Soft cotton material with a few drops of refined linseed oil to moisten. This oily rag will collect all the fine dust left on the wood surface after sanding.
SPONGE STICK Use a sponge stick (a square sponge atop a wooden handle) as a brush to basecoat your piece and to add the final protective coat of varnish. The sponge stick will not leave brush marks.
POLY SPONGE A piece of sponge, preferably round (natural or synthetic sponge is suitable), used for marbling techniques.
FABRIC TOWEL AND COTTON RAGS Painters always have a need for a rag or two.
WET PALETTE In a warm climate the acrylic paints dry very fast. I use what I call a wet palette — a rectangular shallow clear plastic container, with a lid to seal it. Cut a flat cleaning sponge 1–2 cm (½ in) thick to fit inside the base of the container.

Before starting painting, wet the sponge, squeeze out most of the water and place it inside the container. Cut a piece of waxed paper to fit over the sponge, and place your paint in puddles onto the paper. If the phone rings or you must leave your painting, simply cover the wet palette with the lid, and it will keep moist for weeks.

3 Basic Brushstrokes

Please look at the colour worksheets at the front of this book (pages 6 to 10).

All designs for folk art are made with simple brushstrokes, the most common being the 'comma'. The placement and joining of each comma forms the petals of flowers in many designs. The comma stroke is painted with a round brush, the size of brush depending on the size of the area you are painting.

To practise the brushstrokes, place greaseproof paper over the colour worksheets of strokes printed in this book, and paint the different strokes. (Alternatively, photocopy a sheet at an increased size and work from this.) With a little practice each week, you will soon master the technique and begin painting your first piece. Always remember, the most difficult decision to make is *to start*.

LOADING THE BRUSH WITH ONE COLOUR

Loading the Round Brush

For all strokes, hold the brush on the metal part, with the same pressure you would use when writing with a pencil or pen. Gently pat the brush in the paint puddle, pressing softly up and down to fill the brush with paint. Roll the brush on the palette to remove excess paint.

Comma

A round brush, size No. 4, is used for these strokes. It is always advisable to practise first on white paper. With the brush loaded, rest your hand on the surface of the paper, touch the brush to the surface, push down on the brush to fan out the bristles, release the pressure and slowly pull the brush down, lifting it at the same time so that you watch the bristles gradually return to a fine point. Take your time with this brushstroke, as it needs a little control to achieve the fine point at the end of the stroke.

RIGHT-SIDE COMMA Touch the loaded brush to the surface, push down on the brush to fan out the bristles, release the pressure and slowly curve the brush to the right, lifting it at the same time and watching the bristles come slowly back to a fine point.

LEFT-SIDE COMMA As for the right-hand comma but curve the brush to the left.

Leaf Shape

Load the brush with paint, touch the brush to the surface, starting with a very fine line; slowly push down on the brush, pull itdown gently, release the pressure and allow the bristles to return to a fine point.

'S' Shape

Load the brush with paint, touch the brush to the surface, starting with a very fine line; slowly add pressure and at the same time form an 'S' shape, then slowly release the pressure to allow the bristles to return to a fine point at the end of the stroke. A reverse 'S' shape is done the same way.

'C' or Crescent Shape

Load the brush with paint, steady your hand, touch the brush to the surface, starting with a very fine line; turn it to the left, increasing the pressure, then slowly release the pressure and curve the brush back to form a 'C' or crescent shape. A reverse 'C' shape is done the same way.

LOADING THE BRUSH WITH A SECOND COLOUR

Top-loading the Round Brush

Traditional folk art was quite often painted with two colours on the brush at the same time. The technique gives a beautiful effect of depth to the painting. Load your brush first with one colour, then gently lay the tip of the brush into a second colour; turn the brush over, and make a comma stroke on your palette. This opens up the bristles of

the brush. Now with the second colour on the tip of the brush showing (not under the brush), make your stroke in the design. You will need to reload your brush for each stroke. Do not paint over any of these strokes, as you would blend the colours together and lose the effect.

Loading a Flat Brush

A flat or shader brush can be used to make the same strokes as discussed above for a round brush. However, the flat shape of the brush allows the paint to blend across the fibres, so that when you load the brush with the colour on the side and make a stroke you will see a more realistic blend of colours.

Side or Single-loading the Flat Brush

Place a puddle of paint on your palette. Gently pull one side of your brush through the side of the puddle. Blend the colour by stroking the brush on a clean section of your palette until you can see the colour blending through to the centre of the brush's fibres.

Double Side-loading

This is when you have two colours on your flat brush, one on each side of the brush. First, load the brush with one colour on one side. Then pull the other side of the brush into a second colour. Gently stroke on a clean section of palette until both colours blend together. Keep stroking on one spot of the palette until you achieve the desired blend. Try to avoid a striped effect; keep stroking until the centre is blended.

Paint Consistency for a Flat Brush

To paint with a flat brush the paint must have a thin consistency. A medium (such as FolkArt™ Extender) should be added to the paint if it starts to become thick.

Making a Wash or Shading

To make a wash, side-load a wet flat brush in paint. Blend on the palette to allow the colour to run through. One side of the brush must remain free of paint. The process is similar to that of single-loading (above).

SCRIPT LINER BRUSH

Scrolls
Fine Lines

The brush to use for these strokes is a No. 2 Script liner. Load the brush with a very thin paint mix (add water to the paint or use a brand of thin paint). Starting at the inside of a curve, pull a fine line curving either right or left to form an 'M' or 'W' shape, which ends in a small circle. This technique takes a little practice. It is best to hold the brush very firmly, with your hand still, so that you move your whole arm from the shoulder in a curving motion.

4 Preparation of Surfaces

Not all of the following surfaces are covered in this book. However, all the patterns in the book can be used on any of these surfaces.

New Wood

With fine sandpaper (400–1200 grit) sand lightly following the grain of the timber. Remove all the sand dust with a tack cloth (cotton cloth with a few drops of linseed oil). When you sand a large item or more than one item, always wear a safety mask.

Coat the item with a thin coating of FolkArt™ Satin Finish Water Base Varnish; when dry, sand lightly with fine sandpaper. Then apply two coats of your chosen base colour; when dry, sand lightly. Next apply a thin coat of Satin Finish Water Base Varnish over the base colour. This final coat allows you to remove the acrylic paint when you are painting, if marked by accident.

Old Wood, Unpainted

Using a medium-grit sandpaper, sand the complete surface. Next, wash with very hot soapy water to which a little vinegar has been added, to remove the grease in the wood. If there are any holes or cracks in the wood, fill with a wood filler that matches the colour of the timber; when

dry, sand the wood filler. Apply one coat of Satin Finish Water Base Varnish and allow to dry. Apply two coats of the base colour; when dry, sand lightly. Then apply the final thin coat of Satin Finish Water Base Varnish, before you begin painting the folk art pattern.

Metal

(This includes copper, tin, brass, steel.) Wash the item with hot water and detergent, and clean thoroughly with a coarse handbrush. When dry, wash in a mixture of half water and half vinegar to remove any trace of grease or oil on the metal. If the item shows any sign of rust, seal with a rust preventative. (Use this cleaning procedure, even if you do not need to use a rust preventative.)

Apply two coats of Satin Finish Water Base Varnish on the prepared surface; allow to dry overnight, preferably in a warm place. Then apply a basecoat in your chosen colour with two to three coats of paint. Finally apply a thin coat of Satin Finish Water Base Varnish before you start painting the folk art decoration.

Metal is a hard surface, so you must treat it carefully because knocks or bumps will chip the painted surface, even after many coats of paint. Paint on a metal surface needs a lot longer time to cure –

that is, dry and harden. A small metal item can be cured or the drying time quickened by placing it in the oven at 100°C (212°F, or 'cool' setting) for 20 minutes.

Terracotta or Clay

There are many ways to prepare a terracotta or clay surface. For example, as these surfaces are porous, they can be painted on without a sealer. If the item is new, wipe it carefully to remove the dust. If the item is old, wash it in hot soapy water with a little vinegar to remove all traces of dirt and grease.

For a garden pot, with the surface so porous, it is best to keep the plant in its plastic container and just sit the plastic container inside the decorated pot. Then the painted surface will not be marked by water seeping through the walls of the pot.

Apply two coats of the basecoat colour, although maybe three coats will be necessary. I find that FolkArt™ BaseCoat is excellent for pots, as it has a varnish combined with the acrylic paint and makes a good cover. When the final basecoat is totally dry, paint a thin coating of Satin Finish Water Base Varnish.

Bisque Porcelain

Lightly sand any rough edges on the porcelain joins, and wipe with a moist rag to remove dust. Apply two or three coats of the base colour. Finally, apply a thin coat of Satin Finish Water Base Varnish.

Glass or Highly Glazed Surfaces

When painting on glass or a highly glazed surface, you must treat the finished piece as a purely decorative item, because washing in detergents and general handling will eventually chip the painted area. Decide what area of the glass surface is to be decorated and coat only this area with the Satin Finish Water Base Varnish. When it is dry, paint your design. Allow to dry, then seal with a high gloss varnish. Remember that glass is a transparent material and your pattern will be seen from the back as well, so paint neatly.

Paper

There is no special preparation for paper – you can paint directly onto the surface. For cards and bookmarks a thin coat of Satin Finish Water Base Varnish will protect the painted surface.

Candles and Soaps

Apply a thin coat of Satin Finish Water Base Varnish, then paint your design. When dry, apply a final coat of varnish.

Fabric

You will need to buy a textile medium (with instructions for mixing) to add to your acrylic paints for fabric painting. First, wash the item thoroughly to remove any sizing from the fabric. Mix the textile medium with your acrylic paints, as directed for the type of acrylic paint you are using. Once the design is finished, allow to dry overnight. Then heat-set with a warm iron, placing brown paper between the painted surface and the iron.

5 Wood Staining and Antiquing

Always wear rubber gloves when using wood stains.

Water-based Stain

You can make wood stains to match different timber colours using FolkArt™ Acrylic Color. For example, the formulation for a walnut colour is:

> 1 part Satin Finish Water Base Varnish
> 1 part FolkArt™ Acrylic Color Nutmeg

Sand the timber piece with fine-grade sandpaper. Rub with a tack cloth to remove fine dust.

On your palette place one part of Satin Finish Water Base Varnish and one part of your choice of colour; add a small amount of FolkArt™ Extender to give yourself extra time before the wood stain starts to dry. Test the colour mixture on a sample piece of wood before you proceed to stain your item.

Apply the stain with a sponge, working quickly and following the grain of the timber. Stain one section at a time until complete. When totally dry, apply a thin coat of Satin Finish Water Base Varnish before you begin your folk art painting.

Oil-based Stain

Combine the first two ingredients and store in a sealed container:

> 1 part refined linseed oil
> 3 parts gum turpentine
> small amount of artists' oil paint
> (applied direct from tube)

The 'earth colours' of oil paint are used for wood stains:

> Burnt Umber for the colour of walnut
> Raw Sienna for the colour of oak
> Burnt Umber plus Burgundy for dark mahogany

Sand the timber piece with fine-grade sandpaper. Rub with a tack cloth to remove fine dust. Make a ball shape with a soft cotton rag, and apply the mixture of refined linseed oil and gum turpentine to the surface. Select the appropriate colour of artists' oil paint and add a small amount to the moist rag; gently rub onto the timber, following the grain. Some areas will show darker, but this is normal as the timber has varied textures. If the colour is too dark, add more of the refined linseed oil and gum turpentine mixture to dilute the colour. Proceed to stain the whole timber piece. Allow several days for drying, until it is dry when touched. Before painting your design, apply a thin coat of Satin Finish Water Base Varnish.

Antiquing

'Antiquing' creates the old stained colour of timber or metal achieved naturally by generations of household cooking and polishing. My antiquing method uses the same ingredients as for oil-based wood staining:

1 part refined linseed oil
3 parts gum turpentine
small amount of Burnt Umber artists' oil paint

When your design has been completed and is totally dry, apply a thin coat of Satin Finish Water Base Varnish. Allow to dry. Moisten a cotton rag with the refined linseed oil and gum turpentine mixture and rub over the surface, then apply a small amount of the oil paint to the moist rag and cover the surface. If the colour is too strong, apply the mixture to a clean section of the rag, and wipe off any excess oil paint. Also remove the oil paint from the highlighted or white painted areas of the design to create depth in the pattern. Allow a week for the piece to dry, and then coat with Satin Finish Water Base Varnish.

6 Hints for Painting the Design

Have a comfortable area for painting, with plenty of natural light. Painting at night in artificial light is not advisable, because the colours mixed at night will differ from those mixed during daylight hours.

Allow yourself at least two hours for painting. This is usually long enough, for if you become tired it will show in your painting. Paint when you feel like painting, even if you've started on some other chore. You'll find you enjoy your painting more, and the break from your busy schedule will revive you.

Check that the item is completely dry. Sand the surface lightly with fine sandpaper (400–1200 grit), and remove all dust with a moist cloth.

Transfer the pattern of your design onto the item using transfer paper, or sketch your design freehand.

I begin by painting the leaves first, and all the fine stems. Next I do the main flowers and then the 'fillers' and the rest of the design. The borders are the final part I paint.

On your palette, make the puddles of paint in circles about 2.5 cm (1 in) across; if the puddles are smaller, the paint will dry too quickly. When the paint does start to dry mix a few drops of medium (or water) into the puddle to soften the paint. If the paint starts to form a skin on the surface, make a new puddle of fresh paint. In hot weather, use a wet palette (see page 22).

Keep the metal part of your brush dry after rinsing in water; it is important to have a firm grip on the brush. To control your brushstrokes, steady your painting hand with the other hand.

Transferring the Patterns

If a pattern printed in this book is not the exact size you want for painting the design, you will need to enlarge or reduce it. Many photocopying machines can do this task at the touch of a button.

There are two methods for transferring the pattern onto the item to be painted:

1. Use transfer paper, which can be bought from a craft or art supply shop. Several colours are available. First, photocopy the pattern and enlarge or reduce to the desired size. Place the chalk side of the transfer paper onto the face of your piece and tape it down. Then place the pattern on top of the transfer paper, centering the design, and tape it down. Using your stylus, gently trace over the pattern lines, checking to see if the lines are being transferred onto your piece. Do not apply too much pressure, especially with a timber piece, as the lines will indent the timber.

2. Trace the pattern onto tracing paper, then go over the back of the tracing paper with chalk. Place the tracing paper in position with the chalky side against your item, and go over all the elements of the pattern with a stylus. When you've finished painting and the paint is dry, the chalk lines can be easily removed with a damp cotton cloth.

Creating Your Own Patterns

Do use my patterns as a guide, but once you gain confidence, start to create your own designs, gathering inspiration from gift cards, patterns on fabrics, porcelain plates, and so on. Take a closer look at the natural world, and you will soon realise there is a world of patterns all around you.

Freehand Sketching

During classes, I encourage my students to draw their patterns freehand onto their item using a sharpened chalk or chalk pencil. Most students come to me, with the same tale: 'I cannot draw and I am not creative'. I explain to them that if they can hold a pencil, they can draw. They just need encouragement and help to guide them in the right direction.

When drawing a design freehand onto your item it is only necessary to draw the main shapes: a circle for a flower, a triangle shape for a leaf, and so on. Simple shapes for you to follow when painting. The pattern will not be exactly as the original, but this is a step towards making your own designs in the future.

All my students over a seven-week period learn to draw their patterns freehand, and I hope they will go on to actually paint freehand. The joy of teaching is watching students slowly gain confidence and fall in love with this wonderful art.

Trace if you must, but try to draw freehand so that you'll soon be creating your own original folk art.

Colour

Traditional folk art was painted in mainly three colours: red, blue and very dark green. The early folk artists were self-taught, and their designs and colours did not follow the conventional styles of the fine artists, who had the benefit of being shown by the master painters.

With modern folk art we know how to incorporate many more colours and values of the colours into our painting to give a realistic and softer look to our work.

Colour is really up to the individual painter, but it is very important as it is colour that we notice first when attracted to a painted piece, before we look for the detail.

Mixing Your Own Colours

As you become more confident with your folk art, you may wish to mix your own colours from the primary colours: red, yellow and blue.

A combination of any two primary colours will produce a secondary colour: green, orange and violet (or purple). To mix a green, you will need blue and yellow; to lighten the green, you can add white. Orange is a mix of red and yellow. Violet is a mix of red and blue.

A combination of a primary colour with a secondary colour will produce an intermediate colour; red-orange, yellow-orange, yellow-green, blue-green, blue-violet, red-violet. Incidentally, when more than four colours are mixed together, the result is what we call a brown mud.

Terms to Describe Colour

The *value* of a colour is a gauge of how light or dark it is. (To lighten the value of a colour, add white paint.) *Temperature* is easy to remember; the colour is described as being warm or cool. The *hue* is the name of the colour. The brightness or darkness of a colour is what we call the *intensity*.

Painting Scenes with Acrylics

Scenes in folk art are fun to paint. They are not meant to be realistic, so we do not have to concern ourselves with shadows and highlights, or perspective. Every scene you paint will be different. (I can never paint the same scene twice.)

The size of the brush will vary according to the size of the scene, for example, for a brooch, size No. 2 would be appropriate; for a plate, size No. 6 and for furniture, or anything larger, a size No. 10.

When beginning a scene, start with the background and finish at the foreground. Using a flat brush, the size according to the size of the scene, paint the sky, then the highest ridge of mountains, followed by the next row of hills, until gradually the whole area is covered.

When this paint is completely dry, you can begin to paint the detail of the design. A stipple or deerfoot brush is used to paint the trees and shrubs. Cutting the top off an old round brush makes a good stipple brush. To give buildings a contrast and softer look, always shade the edge of the walls with a darker colour.

PART TWO
PROJECTS TO PAINT

Heart-Shaped Belt Buckle

(Photograph page 1)

Sponge marbling is fun to do and makes an interesting background for sprays of roses on this belt buckle.

Base colour   FolkArt™ BaseCoat: Cherry Royale.

Paint   FolkArt™ Acrylic Colors: Taffy, Paisley Blue, Evergreen, Wicker White, Huckleberry, School Bus Yellow, Metallic Pure Gold.

Varnish   FolkArt™ Satin Finish Water Base Varnish, FolkArt™ Hi-Shine Brilliant Glaze.

Brushes   No. 3 round, No. 2 liner.

Other materials   FolkArt™ Extender, poly sponge for marbling, transfer paper, stylus.

Preparation   Refer to instructions for preparation of wood (page 26). Basecoat the whole buckle with Cherry Royale, and allow to dry.

Sponge marbling   Place on your palette separate puddles of Taffy and Paisley Blue. Take a dry sponge, dab it in the Extender to absorb a small amount, then in Taffy, and a little of the Paisley Blue; dab the sponge on the palette to remove excess paint, then proceed to sponge the buckle, allowing a little of the base colour to show through. When dry, apply a thin coat of Satin Finish Water Base Varnish and allow to dry. Transfer the pattern.

Leaves   Load No. 3 round brush with Evergreen, top-load with Wicker White, and paint the leaves.

Stems   Load No. 2 liner brush with Huckleberry and paint stems.

Roses   Load the No. 3 round brush with Cherry Royale, top-load with Wicker White, and paint the roses and rosebuds as shown on the colour worksheet (see page 10). Paint petals with comma strokes.

Daisies   Using the stylus, make Wicker White dots for the daisy petals. Make centre dot with School Bus Yellow. Paint dots for fillers.

Gold border   Load No. 3 round brush with Metallic Pure Gold, and paint commas around the border.

Finish   Varnish with FolkArt™ Hi-Shine Brilliant Glaze.

Oval Belt Buckle

(Photograph page 1)

This timber belt buckle looks beautiful at the waistline, and is also an interesting fastener for a scarf.

Base colour   FolkArt™ BaseCoat: Indigo.
Paint   FolkArt™ Acrylic Colors: Bayberry, Wicker White, School Bus Yellow, Metallic Pure Gold.
Brush   No. 3 round.
Varnish   FolkArt™ Satin Finish Water Base Varnish, FolkArt™ Hi-Shine Brilliant Glaze.
Other materials   White transfer paper, stylus.

Preparation   Refer to instructions for preparation of wood (page 26). Apply Indigo basecoat, and allow to dry. Apply thin coat of Satin Finish Water Base Varnish, and allow to dry. Transfer the pattern.

Leaves and flowers   Load the No. 3 round brush with Bayberry, top-load with Wicker White, and paint the leaves. Using the stylus make Wicker White dots for the daisy petals. Make centre dot with School Bus Yellow.

Border   Make a border of dots with Metallic Pure Gold.

Finish   Varnish with FolkArt™ Hi-Shine Brilliant Glaze.

Round Marbled Brooch

(Photograph page 1)

On this distinctive brooch, the marbled edge complements the design of poppies and small daisies.

Base colour   FolkArt™ BaseCoat: Bottle Green.

Paint   FolkArt™ Acrylic Colors: Shamrock, Wicker White, Spanish Tile, School Bus Yellow, Huckleberry.

Varnish   FolkArt™ Satin Finish Water Base Varnish, FolkArt™ Hi-Shine Brilliant Glaze.

Brushes   Stipple or deer-foot brush, No. 3 round, No. 2 liner.

Other materials   White transfer paper, stylus.

Preparation   Refer to instructions for preparation of wood (page 26). Apply Bottle Green basecoat, and allow to dry. Apply thin coat of Satin Finish Water Base Varnish, and allow to dry. Transfer the pattern.

Marbled edge   Load the deer-foot or stipple brush with Shamrock and Wicker White, and stipple around the edge of the brooch. Reapply basecoat to central area after marbling if you have paint spatters.

Leaves   Load No. 3 round brush with Shamrock, top-load with Wicker White, and paint the leaves.

Stems   Load No. 2 liner brush with Huckleberry, top-load with Wicker White and paint the stems.

Poppies   Load No. 3 round brush with Wicker White, and paint the back of the petals of the poppies. Load the brush with Spanish Tile, and pull white paint down to the centre of each poppy, as shown on the colour worksheet (page 10). In the centre of the flowers, make dots with School Bus Yellow and Huckleberry.

Daisies   Using the stylus, make Wicker White dots for the daisy petals. Make centre dot with School Bus Yellow.

Finish   Apply either a high-gloss varnish or a satin-finish varnish.

Heart-Shaped Brooch

(Photograph page 1)

A hand-painted brooch makes a delightful personalised gift. I cannot resist painting them whenever I have a few spare moments.

Base colour   FolkArt™ BaseCoat: Licorice.

Paint   FolkArt™ Acrylic Colors: Metallic Pure Gold, Evergreen, Wicker White, Calico Red, Paisley Blue, School Bus Yellow.

Varnish   FolkArt™ Satin Finish Water Base Varnish, FolkArt™ Hi-Shine Brilliant Glaze.

Brushes   No. 4 flat, No. 2 round, No. 1 liner.

Other materials   White transfer paper, stylus.

Preparation   Refer to instructions for preparation of wood (page 26). Apply Licorice basecoat, and allow to dry. Apply a thin coat of Satin Finish Water Base Varnish, and allow to dry. Transfer the pattern.

Gold border   Using No. 4 flat brush, side-load with Metallic Pure Gold, and paint the lace border, holding the brush so that the gold paint is applied to the inside of each curve. Load the stylus with paint, and dot the edge of the lace.

Leaves   Load No. 2 round brush with Evergreen, top-load with Wicker White, and paint the leaves. Load No. 1 liner brush with Evergreen, top-load with Wicker White, and paint the stems.

Roses   Load No. 2 round brush with Calico Red, paint the rose shapes, and allow to dry. Load the brush with Calico Red, top-load with Wicker White, and paint comma strokes to form the petals.

Bow   Load No. 1 liner brush with Paisley Blue, top-load with Wicker White, and paint the bow.

Daisies   Using the stylus, make Wicker White dots for the daisy petals. Make centre dot with School Bus Yellow.

Finish   Varnish with FolkArt™ Hi-Shine Brilliant Glaze.

Daisy Bracelet

(Photograph page 1)

Repeat this pattern
around the bracelet

A chain of daisies and blue flowers is easy to paint. This pretty pattern can be used as a border on other items, too.

Base colour   FolkArt™ BaseCoat: Licorice.

Paint   FolkArt™ Acrylic Colors: Bayberry, Wicker White, School Bus Yellow, Huckleberry, Paisley Blue.

Varnish   FolkArt™ Satin Finish Water Base Varnish.

Brushes   No. 3 round, No. 2 liner.

Other materials   White transfer paper, stylus.

Preparation   Refer to instructions for preparation of wood (page 26). Apply Licorice basecoat and allow to dry. Apply a thin coat of Satin Finish Water Base Varnish, and allow to dry. Transfer the pattern.

Leaves   Load No. 3 round brush with Bayberry, top-load with Wicker White, and paint the leaves. Load No. 2 liner brush with Bayberry, top-load with School Bus Yellow, and paint the stems..

Daisies   Load No. 3 round brush with Wicker White, and paint comma strokes for the daisy petals. Load No. 3 round brush with Huckleberry, top-load with School Bus Yellow, and dab in the daisy centres.

Blue flowers   Load the stylus with Paisley Blue, and dot in the flower petals. In the centre, make a dot with School Bus Yellow.

Finish   Varnish with FolkArt™ Satin Finish Water Base Varnish.

Roses and Berries Bracelet

(Photograph page 1)

Repeat this pattern around the bracelet

Unlike most folk art that is rarely seen beyond the home, decorated bracelets and bangles can give pleasure to a wider audience. This roses and berries bracelet blends with many of the clothes I wear.

Base colour   FolkArt™ BaseCoat: Indigo.

Paint   FolkArt™ Acrylic Colors: Poppy Seed, Bayberry, Mystic Green, Cherry Royale, Wicker White, Prairie Blue, Licorice, Wild Rose, School Bus Yellow.

Varnish   FolkArt™ Satin Finish Water Base Varnish, FolkArt™ Hi-Shine Brilliant Glaze.

Brushes   No. 4 flat, No. 6 flat, No. 2 liner.

Other materials   Sponge stick, fine sandpaper, white transfer paper, chalk, stylus.

Preparation   Using a sponge stick or large brush, apply two coats of Indigo basecoat, allowing time for each coat to dry. Sand lightly for a smooth finish. Apply a thin coat of Satin Finish Water Base Varnish, and allow to dry. Transfer the pattern.

Leaves   Using No. 6 flat brush, double-load with Poppy Seed and Bayberry (see the instructions for double-loading and side-loading a flat brush, page 24). Paint large leaves next to the rose. Load No. 2 liner brush with Mystic Green, and paint the fine scrolled lines near the edges of the leaves.

Rose   Using No. 6 flat brush, double-load with Cherry Royale and Wicker White, carefully blending the colour through the brush's fibres, and paint the back petals at the top of the rose. Continue to paint the rose, as shown on the colour worksheet (page 8).

Berries   Load No. 4 flat brush with

Prairie Blue, and paint the berries. Using chalk, re-trace the small round circles of individual berries. Side-load the brush with Licorice, and shade the left side of the small chalk circles. Then load the brush with Wicker White, and highlight the right side of each chalk circle. Using a stylus, place a small white dot in each circle. Load No. 4 flat brush with Mystic Green, side-load with Wild Rose, and paint small leaves under the berries.

White flower   Load No. 4 flat brush with Wicker White, and paint small crescents for each petal. In the centre, use a stylus to make a small dot of School Bus Yellow. Using your stylus, paint graduated dots in Wicker White leading away from the white flower.

Finish   Varnish with FolkArt™ Hi-Shine Brilliant Glaze.

Ceramic Daisy Duck

(Photograph page 3)

Pattern for head of duck

Pattern for neck of duck

Pattern around base of duck

This pottery duck was made by a student in my folk art class. I hope she likes the pattern I have designed for it. Ceramics are a wonderfully smooth surface to paint on.

Base colour   FolkArt™ BaseCoat: Bottle Green.

Paint   FolkArt™ Acrylic Colors: Fresh Foliage, School Bus Yellow, Wicker White, Spanish Tile, Cherry Royale, Licorice, Paisley Blue, Huckleberry.

Varnish   FolkArt™ Satin Finish Water Base Varnish.

Brushes   No. 5 round, No. 2 liner, No. 4 flat.

Other materials   White transfer paper, stylus.

Preparation   Apply two coats of Bottle Green basecoat. When dry, apply a thin coat of Satin Finish Water Base Varnish. When dry, transfer the pattern. The main pattern is repeated on the back of the duck.

Leaves   Load No. 5 round brush with Fresh Foliage, top-load with School Bus Yellow, and paint the large leaves. Load the brush with Fresh Foliage, top-load with Wicker White, and paint smaller leaves. Using No. 2 liner brush, paint thin stems from the flowers and small leaves.

Daisies   Load No. 5 round brush with Spanish Tile, top-load with Wicker White, and paint comma strokes for the petals, pulling from the outside of each petal into the centre of the daisy. Load the brush with Cherry Royale, top-load with School Bus Yellow, and dab in the centre of each daisy. Using the stylus, make dots of Licorice and Wicker White in the centre (over the previous colour).

Blue flowers   Using No. 4 flat brush, side-load with Paisley Blue, blend, then load the opposite side of the brush with Wicker White and gently blend; paint small crescent shapes for the flower tubes,

Pattern for front of duck

placing the lighter colour on the brush at the top of each crescent. Using the stylus, dot Wicker White at the top of each flower tube. Load No. 2 liner brush with Huckleberry and paint the fine stems.

Scroll border   Mix a pale yellow with Wicker White and a little School Bus Yellow. Load No. 5 round brush with the pale yellow, top-load with Wicker White, and paint a series of commas as shown on the pattern. Trim with Wicker White dots,

using the wooden end of your brush.

Ribbon trim   Using No. 2 liner brush, load with Fresh Foliage, top-load with Wicker White, and paint the ribbon and bow.

Little red daisies   Using the stylus, make Spanish Tile dots for the petals. Make centre dot with School Bus Yellow.

Finish   Varnish with FolkArt™ Satin Finish Water Base Varnish.

Oval Timber Box

(Photograph page 3)

This fine timber box can be used for many things: to store your favourite cards, your sewing cottons and threads, or note paper and pens. The crisp traditional design looks good in any room.

Base colour   FolkArt™ BaseCoat: Indigo.

Paint   FolkArt™ Acrylic Colors: Green Olive, Wicker White, School Bus Yellow, Huckleberry, Cherry Royale, Licorice, Plum Pudding, Paisley Blue, Buttercup, Metallic Pure Gold.

Varnish   FolkArt™ Satin Finish Water Base Varnish.

Brushes   No. 5 round, No. 2 liner.

Other materials   Sponge stick or large brush for basecoat, white transfer paper, stylus.

Preparation   Refer to instructions for preparation of wood (page 26). Apply Indigo basecoat to entire box, inside and out. When dry, transfer the pattern.

Leaves   Load No. 5 round brush with Green Olive, top-load with Wicker White, and paint the large leaves. Load the brush with Green Olive, top-load with School Bus Yellow, and paint smaller leaves. Using No. 2 liner, paint the stems with Huckleberry and paint the scrolls with Green Olive.

Daisies   Load No. 5 round brush with Wicker White, and paint comma strokes for the petals, pulling from the outside of each petal into the centre of the daisy. Load the brush with Huckleberry, top-load with School Bus Yellow, and dab in the centre of each daisy. Using the stylus, dot with Wicker White.

Rose   Using No. 5 round brush, paint the rose area with Cherry Royale. Shade with Licorice. Load the brush with Cherry Royale, top-load with Wicker White and paint commas outlining the petals, as shown on the colour worksheet on page 10.

Poppy   Load the brush with Plum Pudding, top-load with Wicker White, and paint the petals (refer to the colour worksheet page 10). Paint the centre with Huckleberry, and make dots with School Bus Yellow. Load the brush with Green Olive, top-load with Huckleberry, and paint the stem.

Small blue flowers   Load No. 5 round brush with Paisley Blue, top-load with Wicker White, and paint small crescent strokes for petals. Load the brush with Huckleberry, top-load with School Bus Yellow, and dab in the flower centres. Dot the centres with Wicker White and Licorice, using the wooden end of your brush.

Cream flowers   Load No. 5 round brush with Buttercup, top-load with Wicker White, and paint small crescent strokes for petals. Load the brush with Huckleberry, top-load with School Bus Yellow, and dab in the flower centres. Dot with Wicker White and Licorice.

Border   Load the No. 5 round brush with Metallic Pure Gold, and paint comma strokes. Using the stylus, dot with gold.

Finish   Varnish with FolkArt™ Satin Finish Water Base Varnish.

Pattern for top of Oval Timber Box

Pattern for side panel of Oval Timber Box

Ceramic Decorative Pots

(Photograph page 2)

Two old terracotta pots were looking rather forlorn in my garden, but now with a fresh coat of paint and pretty floral designs they have a new life.

A ceramic pot is porous unless the inside of the pot has been glazed and fired, so any plant must stay in its plastic container when it is placed into the decorated pot.

Base colours   FolkArt™ BaseCoat: Chocolate Parfait for poppy-pattern pot, Porcelain White for daisy-pattern pot.

Paint   FolkArt™ Acrylic Colors: Thicket, Wicker White, School Bus Yellow, Calico Red, Paisley Blue, Chocolate Fudge.

Varnish   FolkArt™ Satin Finish Water Base Varnish.

Brushes   No. 5 round, No. 2 liner.

Other materials   Transfer paper.

Preparation   Refer to instructions for preparation of terracotta or clay (page 27). Apply basecoat over inside and outside of each pot, and allow to dry. Then apply a second coat, and allow to dry. Transfer the patterns.

Poppy pattern

Leaves   Load No. 5 round brush with Thicket, top-load with Wicker White, and paint large leaves. Load the brush with Thicket, top-load with School Bus Yellow, and paint small leaves.

Soft-wheat pattern   Load the brush with School Bus Yellow, top-load with Wicker White, and paint the grains of wheat.

Poppies   No. 5 round brush. Wicker White, Paisley Blue, Calico Red, as shown on the colour worksheet (page 10). For the centre, load the brush with Chocolate Fudge and top-load with School Bus Yellow.

Bow   Load No. 5 brush with Paisley Blue, top-load with Wicker White, and paint the bow.

Borders   Around the top of the pot use No. 2 liner brush to paint the comma pattern with Paisley Blue. Around the lower base of the pot, paint a small leaf stroke. Between the commas and the leaf strokes, use the wooden end of your brush to paint small daisies using Wicker White for petals and School Bus Yellow for the dot centres.

Daisy pattern

Leaves   Load No. 5 round brush with Thicket, top-load with School Bus Yellow, and paint large leaves near the daisy as well as the smaller leaves. Using No. 2 liner brush, paint scrolls and stems for the outer small leaves. Load No. 5 round brush with

Thicket, top-load with Wicker White, and paint the commas above and below the centre daisy.

Flowers   Load No. 5 round brush with Wicker White, and paint comma strokes, pulling from the outer edge into the centre of the daisy. Paint the half daisy the same way. For the base of the half daisy, paint with Thicket top-loaded with School Bus Yellow. For centre of the daisy, load the No. 5 round brush with Chocolate Fudge and

top-load with School Bus Yellow.

Border   Load the brush with Wicker White, top-load with a little School Bus Yellow, and paint the commas. For the dot flowers between commas, use the wooden end of your brush to make petals in Wicker White, and centre dots in School Bus Yellow.

Finish   Varnish both pots with FolkArt™ Satin Finish Water Base Varnish.

Daisy pattern

Poppy pattern

Metal Creamer

(Photograph page 2)

Many dairy farmers will recognise this old creamer. Many folk artists have had a chance to paint one. The larger cans make ideal umbrella holders.

Base colours FolkArt™ BaseCoat: Butter Pecan. FolkArt™ Acrylic Color: Thicket.

Paint FolkArt™ Acrylic Colors: Buttercrunch, Evergreen, School Bus Yellow, Calico Red, Cherry Royale, Wicker White, Huckleberry, Paisley Blue.

Varnish FolkArt™ Satin Finish Water Base Varnish.

Brushes Large bristle brush, No. 5 round, No. 3 round, No. 2 liner.

Other materials Transfer paper, poly sponge (to sponge area under floral bouquet), stylus.

Preparation Refer to instructions for preparation of metal (page 26). Mark out the different areas of the design, and paint Butter Pecan (light areas) and Thicket (dark areas) using the large bristle brush. When dry, apply a thin coat of Satin Finish Water Base Varnish. Allow to dry, then transfer the pattern.

Scroll between base colours Load No. 5 round brush with Buttercrunch, top-load with Wicker White, and paint comma strokes, as well as the spiderweb pattern beneath the vase.

Garland over scrolls Load No. 3 round brush with Evergreen, top-load with School Bus Yellow, and paint the leaves.

Roses Load the No. 3 round brush with Calico Red, and paint the base colour of the rose shapes; allow to dry. Load the brush with Calico Red, top-load with Wicker White, and paint over each rose with comma strokes to form petals. Use No. 2 liner brush loaded with Evergreen to paint stems from the roses.

Dot daisies Using the wooden end of your brush, make Buttercrunch dots for the daisy petals. Make centre dot with Cherry Royale.

Vase of Flowers

Using a poly sponge, load with a little Evergreen and Wicker White, and gently sponge the area for the flowers in the vase. Allow to dry, and re-transfer the flowers' pattern on the sponged area.

Vase Load No. 3 round brush with Huckleberry, top-load with Wicker White, and paint comma strokes to form the shape of the vase.

Leaves Load No. 3 round brush with Evergreen, top-load with School Bus Yellow and paint the leaves.

Roses See the instructions above, for roses in the garland.

Daisy Load No. 3 round brush with Wicker White, and paint the petals. Load the brush with Huckleberry, top-load with School Bus Yellow, and paint the centre.

Blue flowers Using a stylus, make Paisley Blue dots for the petals. Make centre dot with School Bus Yellow. Add more dots in Wicker White to highlight the floral bouquet.

Finish Varnish with FolkArt™ Satin Finish Water Base Varnish.

Pattern for neck of creamer

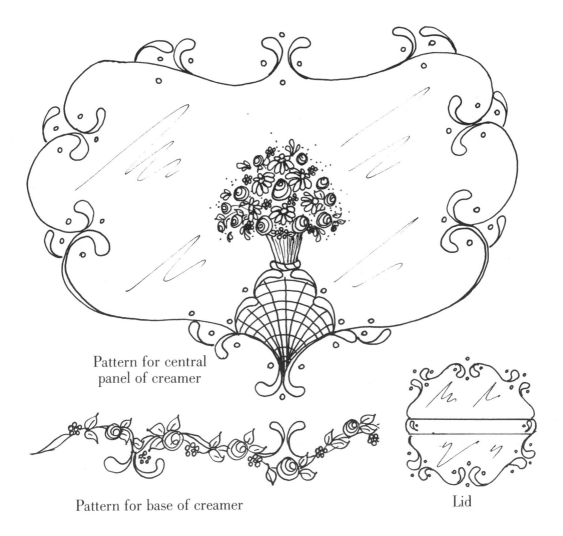

Pattern for central
panel of creamer

Pattern for base of creamer

Lid

Small Wooden Jar

(Photograph page 11)

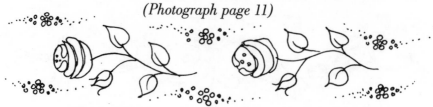

Repeat this pattern around the side of the jar

This beautifully turned wooden jar is decorated with a very easy pattern of rosebuds. This simple design will help the beginner to gain confidence for future painting.

Base colour   FolkArt™ BaseCoat: Bottle Green.

Paint   FolkArt™ Acrylic Colors: Mystic Green, Wicker White, Calico Red, Licorice, School Bus Yellow.

Varnish   FolkArt™ Satin Finish Water Base Varnish.

Brushes   No. 3 round, No. 2 liner.

Other materials   White transfer paper, stylus.

Preparation   Refer to instructions for preparation of timber (page 26). Apply Bottle Green basecoat over the outside of the jar and allow to dry. Apply a thin coat of Satin Finish Water Base Varnish and allow to dry. Transfer the pattern.

Leaves   Load No. 3 round brush with Mystic Green, top-load with Wicker White, and paint the leaves. Load No. 2 liner brush with Mystic Green, top-load with Wicker White, and paint the stems.

Rosebud   Load No. 3 round brush with Calico Red, and paint the rosebud background. Shade the top of the circle and the lower edge in Licorice. Load the brush with Calico Red, top-load with Wicker White, and make comma strokes to form petals on the red background. Using a stylus, place three dots of Wicker White in the centre of the rose.

Dot daisies   Using the stylus, make Wicker White dots for the petals on the jar and lid. Make centre dot with School Bus Yellow.

Dot trim   Make dots around the lid in Wicker White using the stylus.

Finish   Varnish with FolkArt™ Satin Finish Water Base Varnish.

Lid

Wooden Counter Bell

(Photograph page 11)

This little wooden bell sits in my studio, where it acts as a model for some of the first flowers that my students paint. The flowers are my interpretation of a traditional old-fashioned rose. The bell has been antiqued (see page 29).

Base colour   FolkArt™ BaseCoat: Licorice.

Paints   FolkArt™ Acrylic Colors: Evergreen, Wicker White, Taffy, Calico Red, Licorice, Ultramarine.

Varnish   FolkArt™ Satin Finish Water Base Varnish.

Brushes   No. 3 round, No. 2 liner, No. 6 flat.

Other materials   White transfer paper, sponge stick, stylus.

Preparation   Refer to instructions for preparation of wood (page 26). Apply Licorice basecoat, and allow to dry. Transfer the pattern.

Leaves   Load No. 3 round brush with Evergreen, top-load with Wicker White, and paint all leaves.

Filler commas   Load No. 2 liner brush with Taffy, and paint the commas as shown in pattern.

Roses   Load No. 3 round brush with Calico Rose and paint the ball area of the roses. Shade the lower edge of the ball and the top with Licorice. Load No. 3 round brush with Calico Red, top-load with Wicker White, and paint comma strokes over the roses, as shown in the pattern. Dot the dark-shaded centre with Wicker White using the stylus.

Trim Load No. 6 flat brush with Taffy, and paint crescent shapes around the edge and top of the bell. Load No. 2 liner with Taffy, and paint thin lacy lines coming from the edge of the crescents. Using a stylus, make Taffy dots along the edge of the crescents, and where the fine lines meet.

Bow Load No. 2 liner brush with Ultramarine, top-load with Wicker White, and paint small bow around the base of the handle.

Finish Varnish with FolkArt™ Satin Finish Water Base Varnish. When it is completely dry, you may choose to give it an antiquing treatment (see page 29).

Austrian Wooden Plate

(Photograph page 11)

A friend of mine has a fine collection of old prints from Austria, dating from the 1890s, illustrating farmers with their cows and goats. On seeing these, I decided to combine the traditional Bauernmalerei flowers with an Alpine scene of a boy walking his cow and goat to the market.

Base colour   FolkArt™ BaseCoat: Bottle Green.

Paint   FolkArt™ Acrylic Colors: Ultramarine, Wicker White, School Bus Yellow, Licorice, Huckleberry, Calico Red.

Varnish   FolkArt™ Satin Finish Water Base Varnish.

Brushes   No. 6 flat, No. 4 round, No. 2 liner.

Other materials   White transfer paper.

Preparation   Refer to instructions for preparation of wood (page 26). Apply Bottle Green basecoat and allow to dry. Apply a thin coat of Satin Finish Water Base Varnish and allow to dry.

ALPINE SCENE   Using white transfer paper, gently trace the pattern onto the wooden plate. Adjust the placing of the pattern to the size of the plate. Start painting at the top of the scene. Mix a soft sky blue colour from Ultramarine and Wicker White, and using No. 6 flat brush, paint the sky with horizontal flat strokes. Details of clouds are shown in the colour worksheet on page 7.

Distant mountains   Mix a dark green from Ultramarine and School Bus Yellow plus a little Licorice. Paint the mountains.

Rolling hills   Add more yellow to the dark green mixture, and paint the hills. Add even more yellow to make a straw colour for the next row of hills, finishing at the road. The foreground is a pale green mixture.

Ridges on distant mountains   Side-load the No. 6 flat brush with Licorice, and wash the top of the ridges to form peaks of shaded colour.

Distant trees   Mix a dark green from Ultramarine and School Bus Yellow plus a little Licorice. Load No. 4 round brush with dark green, top-load with Wicker White, and dab the treeline along the ridge at the foot of the mountains.

House   Mix a soft cream colour from Wicker White and School Bus Yellow, and paint the side walls using No. 4 round brush. Mix a grey from Licorice and Wicker White, and paint the roof.

Pine trees   Mix a light green, load the brush, top-load with Wicker White, and paint in the pine trees using No. 4 round brush.

Fence   Mix a pale grey, load No. 2 liner brush with it, top-load with Wicker White, and paint the fence.

Cow   Using No. 4 round brush, paint the base area with Wicker White; shade dark areas with Huckleberry; neckband Calico

Pattern for central panel of
Austrian Wooden Plate

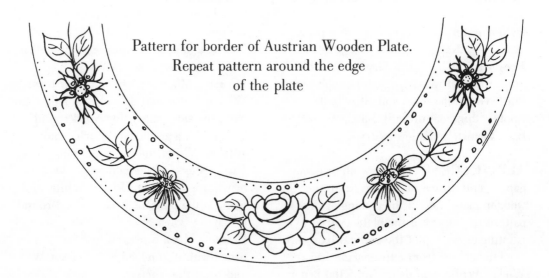

Pattern for border of Austrian Wooden Plate.
Repeat pattern around the edge
of the plate

Red with Wicker White; bell School Bus Yellow.

Farmer boy   Use No. 4 round brush to paint the shoes Licorice, socks Wicker White with Licorice trim, pants in tan made from a mix of Huckleberry, Wicker White and Calico Red, shirt Wicker White, waistcoat Calico Red, hat Licorice, hair Huckleberry.

Goat   Paint the goat with Wicker White, with highlights of Huckleberry using No. 4 round brush. Paint the bell School Bus Yellow, the band Calico Red.

FLOWER BORDER   Mix a soft green from School Bus Yellow, Ultramarine and Wicker White. Load No. 4 round brush with it, top-load with School Bus Yellow, and paint the leaves. Paint the veins in the leaves with Huckleberry.

Roses   Using No. 4 round brush, basecoat Calico Red, shade the top with Huckleberry and paint petals in Calico Red top-loaded with Wicker White, using the comma strokes.

Daisies   Paint the petals Wicker White, with green along the centre. In the centre of each daisy, make dots of Wicker White, School Bus Yellow and Huckleberry. Using No. 2 liner brush with Huckleberry, pull fine lines from the centre, onto each white petal.

Blue flowers   Load No. 4 round brush with Ultramarine, top-load with Wicker White, and paint the petals. Make School Bus Yellow dots for the centre.

Trim   Around the scene and around edge of plate, make graduated dots with Wicker White.

Finish   When totally dry (allow twenty-four hours), apply three coats of Satin Finish Water Base Varnish, allowing adequate drying time between coats.

Wooden Egg

(Photograph page 11)

Scene
and border

Rear
design

This painted wooden egg is in memory of my mother, who loved art and encouraged me to paint.

Base colour FolkArt™ BaseCoat: Licorice.

Paint FolkArt™ Acrylic Colors: Wicker White, Blueberry Pie, Green Olive, Licorice, Apricot Cream, Poppy Seed, School Bus Yellow, Rose Garden, Bayberry, Cherry Royale, Calico Red.

Varnish FolkArt™ Satin Finish Water Base Varnish.

Brushes No. 4 flat, No. 3 round, No. 1 liner.

Other materials Sponge stick, fine sanding paper, white transfer paper, stylus.

Preparation Using a sponge stick or large flat brush apply two coats of Licorice basecoat. Sand lightly when dry. Apply a thin coat of Satin Finish Water Base Varnish. Transfer the pattern using transfer paper or draw freehand.

SCENE Start painting at the top of the scene. Mix a light blue from Wicker White and Blueberry Pie, load No. 4 flat brush, and paint the sky, using horizontal strokes.

56

Load the brush with Green Olive, and paint the hills and the foreground to the lower edge of the scene. When dry, retrace the pattern details.

Clouds Side-load the brush with Wicker White, and wash in crescent shapes over the blue sky.

Foliage Load No. 3 round brush with Green Olive, top-load with a little Licorice, and gently stipple in the details of bushes and grass. When the paint is dry, re-transfer the pattern of the lady.

Lady Using No. 3 round brush, paint the base areas: dress Blueberry Pie, face and arms Apricot Cream with a little Wicker White added, hair Poppy Seed.

Detail of dress Side-load No. 4 flat brush with Licorice, and wash in the folds of the skirt. Load No. 3 round brush with Blueberry Pie, top-load with Wicker White, and paint the scarf as small comma strokes from shoulder to waist, falling over the skirt.

Facial details Load No. 1 liner brush with Poppy Seed, and paint facial details.

Hair details Load No. 3 round brush with Green Olive, top-load with a little School Bus Yellow, and dab in detail on hair. Load No. 1 liner brush with Rose Garden, top-load with Wicker White, and paint the ribbon in the hair.

Necklace Using the stylus, make School Bus Yellow dots, then smaller dots of Licorice.

Bouquet Load No. 3 round brush with Bayberry, top-load with School Bus Yellow, and dab in the leaves. Using a stylus, dot with Calico Red combined with Wicker White for the flowers.

BORDER AND REAR DESIGN

Leaves Load No. 3 round brush with Green Olive, top-load with Wicker White and paint the leaves where shown on the pattern.

Pink roses Load the brush with Cherry Royale, and paint the base colour of the rose shape. Shade the top and lower edge with Licorice. Load the brush with Rose Garden, top-load with Wicker White, and paint over each rose with comma strokes to form petals, as shown on the colour worksheet (page 10). Using the stylus, make Wicker White dots in the centre.

Apricot roses Paint the base with Calico Red. Shade top and lower edge with Licorice. For petals, load the brush with Apricot Cream, top-load with Wicker White. Make Wicker White dots in centre.

Blue daisy Using the stylus make Blueberry Pie and Wicker White dots for petals, and add a School Bus Yellow dot in the centre.

Small yellow daisies Make School Bus Yellow dots for petals, and add a Cherry Royale dot in the centre.

Bow Load No. 3 round brush with Rose Garden, top-load with Wicker White and paint the bow.

Finish Varnish with FolkArt™ Satin Finish Water Base Varnish.

57

Timber Key Holder

(Photograph page 11)

We all need a special place for spare keys. This key holder is a popular item in our studio, and it does make an ideal gift. The painted design is very traditional, incorporating the vase, tulips and daisies, against a warm earth background. It can be used on many different items.

Base colour   FolkArt™ BaseCoat: Rusty Nail.

Paint   FolkArt™ Acrylic Colors: Rusty Nail, Thicket, Harvest Gold, Honeycomb, Brownie, Wicker White, Paisley Blue, Licorice, Plum Pudding, School Bus Yellow, Christmas Red, Glazed Carrots.

Varnish   FolkArt™ Satin Finish Water Base Varnish.

Brushes   No. 3 round, No. 6 flat, No. 2 liner.

Other materials   Tracing paper, stylus.

Preparation   Refer to instructions for preparation of wood (page 26). Apply a basecoat of Rusty Nail, and allow to dry. Paint the outer edge Thicket with No. 6 flat brush. Trim with Harvest Gold using No. 2 liner brush. Transfer the pattern.

Vase   Load No. 6 flat brush with Honeycomb, and paint the vase area. Two coats of paint may be necessary. Using No. 6 flat brush, shade outer edge of vase with Brownie. Load No. 3 round brush with Harvest Gold, top-load with Wicker White, and paint comma strokes.

Leaves   Load No. 3 round brush with Thicket, top-load with Wicker White, and paint the leaves.

Tulips   Load No. 3 round brush with Paisley Blue, top-load with Wicker White, and paint the petals. Mix a blue from Paisley Blue and a little Licorice, and shade the tulip petals, working from the base of each tulip (see page 10).

Mauve daisies   Load No. 3 round brush with Plum Pudding, top-load with Wicker White, and paint petals as comma strokes from the outside of each flower into the centre. Load the brush with Brownie, top-load with School Bus Yellow, and paint the centre. Make Wicker White dots in the centre with the stylus.

Open flowers   Red flower: Paint the flower area with Christmas Red using No. 3 round brush. Load No. 2 liner brush with Harvest Gold, top-load with Wicker White, and paint small comma strokes around the outer edge of the flower. For brushstrokes coming into the centre of the flower, load the brush with Christmas Red and top-load with Wicker White. For the centre, load No. 3 round brush with Brownie and top-load with School Bus Yellow. Make Wicker White dots around the centre. Orange flower: substitute Glazed Carrots for Christmas Red.

Small dot daisies   Using the stylus, make Wicker White dots for the daisy petals. Make centre dot with School Bus Yellow.

Fillers   Load No. 2 liner brush with Harvest Gold, top-load with Wicker White, and paint commas as shown on the pattern.

Finish   Varnish with FolkArt™ Satin Finish Water Base Varnish.

Small Wooden Pan

(Photograph page 11)

This small wooden pan was found in an 'old wares' market. The design is one of the first that I get my students to paint in class. It has the three basic flowers of folk art – the rose, the tulip and the daisy – framed by a border of comma brushstrokes.

Base colour FolkArt™ BaseCoat: Licorice.
Paint FolkArt™ Acrylic Colors: Mystic Green, Wicker White, Taffy, Cherry Royale, Licorice, Ultramarine, School Bus Yellow, Brownie, Buttercup, Bayberry.
Varnish FolkArt™ Satin Finish Water Base Varnish.
Brushes No. 4 round, No. 2 liner.
Other materials Sponge stick or old brush to paint the base colour, stylus, white transfer paper.

Preparation Refer to instructions for preparation of wood (page 26). Apply a Licorice basecoat over the whole item, and allow to dry. Then apply a thin coat of Satin Finish Water Base Varnish, and allow to dry. Transfer the pattern.
Leaves and stems Load No. 2 liner brush with Mystic Green, top-load the brush with Wicker White, and paint thin stems of flowers. With No. 4 round brush, load with Mystic Green, top-load with Wicker White, and paint large leaves and large commas. Clean the brush, load with Taffy, top-load with Wicker White, and paint the small commas.
Rose Paint the rose with Cherry Royale using No. 4 round brush. Shade with Licorice in the centre and lower edge of the rose. Load the brush with Cherry Royale, top-load with Wicker White, and paint commas over the rose to make the petals, as shown on the colour worksheet page 10.
Tulip Paint the base area with Ultramarine, and allow to dry. Prepare a lighter blue by adding a little Wicker White to Ultramarine. Load the brush with this lighter blue, top-load with Wicker White, and paint strokes as shown on the colour worksheet page 10.
Daisy Load No. 4 round brush with Wicker White, and paint comma strokes, pulling into the centre of the daisy. Load tip of brush with a little School Bus Yellow, Wicker White and Brownie, and dab in the centre of the daisy.
Small daisies Using the wooden end of your brush, dip into Wicker White and make small dot petals for each flower. For small leaves, use Mystic Green top-loaded with Wicker White. For centre of daisy, use School Bus Yellow.
Border Paint straight narrow leaf shape with No. 2 liner brush, loaded with Taffy, top-loaded with Wicker White. Paint commas and dots in Buttercup using No. 2 liner brush. Apply Taffy dots in border pattern using the wooden end of your brush.
Handle pattern Paint bands around the handle with Bayberry. Paint dot daisies in Wicker White, with Buttercup centres using stylus.
Finish Varnish with FolkArt™ Satin Finish Water Base Varnish.

Pattern for
design inside pan

Handle trim

Repeat border around the edge of the pan

Old Parlour Heater

(Photograph page 11)

At the end of its useful life as a heater, this was sold at a friend's 'old wares' shop. Folk art has given it a new, more decorative role and, we hope, saved a small piece of our history.

Base colour   FolkArt™ BaseCoat: Licorice.

Paint   FolkArt™ Acrylic Colors: Taffy, Apricot Cream, Wicker White, Shamrock, Bayberry, Harvest Gold, Cherry Royale, Victorian Rose, Lavender Sachet, Nutmeg, Licorice.

Varnish   FolkArt™ Satin Finish Water Base Varnish.

Brushes   No. 3 round, No. 2 liner, No. 5 round, No. 6 flat, No. 4 flat.

Other materials   White transfer paper, stylus.

Preparation   Refer to instructions for preparation of metal (page 26). Apply Licorice basecoat and allow to dry. Apply a thin coat of Satin Finish Water Base Varnish. When dry, transfer the pattern.

Lace borders   Load No. 3 round brush with Taffy, and paint comma strokes, coming from the centre to the outer edge of the lace. Load No. 2 liner brush with Taffy, and paint a thin comma stroke around the curve of the lace. Using a stylus, make Taffy dots along this curve, then paint fine lines curving from the top of the dots. Finish with small dots on the top of these fine lines.

Ribbon   Load No. 5 round brush with Apricot Cream, top-load with Wicker White, and paint ribbons coming from the large rose pattern and also around the small rose border trim.

Leaves   Load No. 5 round brush with Shamrock, top-load with Bayberry, and paint large leaves. Load No. 2 liner brush with Nutmeg, and paint fine veins on the leaves. Load the brush with Shamrock, top-load with Wicker White, and paint the small leaves. Paint the filler leaves with Harvest Gold.

Large rose   Using No. 6 flat brush, paint with flat brush technique (refer to colour worksheet page 8). Colours used: Cherry Royale, side-loaded with Victorian Rose. Highlight in centre of rose with Harvest Gold and Wicker White.

Rose buds   Load No. 4 flat brush with Cherry Royale, side-load with Victorian Rose, and paint a crescent shape for the top of each bud; paint a reverse crescent shape to close the bud. Using No. 2 liner brush in Wicker White, make fine lines coming from the centre of the bud.

Small flowers   Load No. 6 flat brush with Lavender Sachet, side-load in Wicker White, and paint two rows of petals to form each flower. Paint the centres with Harvest Gold, shade with Nutmeg, and highlight with Wicker White. Make dots with Nutmeg, Licorice and Wicker White.

Finish   Varnish with FolkArt™ Satin Finish Water Base Varnish.

Lace trim for base and top of heater

Pattern for central side panel of heater

Middle border
to repeat around the heater

Pattern for leg
of heater

Pattern for top
of heater

Pattern for leg
of heater

Old Dairy Bucket

(Photograph page 12)

Give an old bucket a new lease of life with a coat of paint and a floral decoration, and it becomes quite useful in the home. Store newspapers, wood or umbrellas, or use it as a wastepaper bin in the bathroom. I recommend that you give it an antiquing treatment as I have done, in keeping with the bucket's age.

Base colour   FolkArt™ BaseCoat: Bottle Green.

Paint   FolkArt™ Acrylic Colors: Evergreen, School Bus Yellow, Huckleberry, Blueberry Pie, Wicker White, Spanish Tile, Plum Pudding, Licorice, Calico Red.

Varnish   FolkArt™ Satin Finish Water Base Varnish.

Brushes   No. 5 round, No. 2 liner, No. 3 round.

Other materials   Chalk, poly sponge, white transfer paper, stylus.

Preparation   Refer to instructions for preparation of metal (page 26). Apply Bottle Green basecoat and allow to dry. Decide where you are going to put the floral bouquet, and mark this area with chalk. Lightly sponge this area with Evergreen using a poly sponge. Allow to dry, then transfer the pattern onto the prepared area.

Leaves   Load No. 5 round brush with Evergreen, top-load with School Bus Yellow, and paint leaves using a comma stroke. Load No. 2 liner brush with Huckleberry and paint stems and veins on leaves.

Bow of bouquet   Load No. 5 round brush with Blueberry Pie, top-load with Wicker White, and paint ribbons and bow.

White daisies   Load No. 5 round brush with Wicker White, and paint leaf strokes for the petals. Load the brush with Huckleberry, top-load with School Bus Yellow, and dab in the daisy centre.

Small apricot bells   Load No. 3 round brush with Spanish Tile, top-load with Wicker White, paint comma strokes from the stem of the bell to the edge.

Filler flowers   Load No. 3 round brush with Plum Pudding, top-load with Wicker White, and dab the two colours along the side of the stem. Dot the top of each petal with Licorice.

Rose   Load No. 5 round brush with Calico Red, and paint the base of the rose shape; allow to dry. Load the brush with Calico Red, top-load with Wicker White, and paint over each rose with comma strokes to form the petals. Load the wooden end of the brush with School Bus Yellow, and swirl a circle in the centre of each rose.

Border   Load No. 5 round brush with Wicker White, and paint a series of comma strokes.

Small bows   Load No. 3 round brush with Blueberry Pie, top-load with Wicker

Pattern for borders and central design

Bows are casually placed
over the bucket wherever
desired, between the
two central images

White, and paint the bows around the bucket. Using a stylus, paint dot daisies in the centre of each bow, some in Wicker White, some in Calico Red and some in Spanish Tile.

Finish Varnish with FolkArt™ Satin Finish Water Base Varnish. When it is completely dry, if desired, you may give it an antiquing treatment (see page 29).

Antiqued Coal-Scuttle

(Photograph page 12)

Coal-scuttles have been used for almost three centuries to carry coal to fireplaces within the home. This almost-cylindrical shape helps make a floral design easy to paint. The antiquing process will give the artwork a patina of old age and promote the container to a less-utilitarian role where it won't be subjected to rough handling.

Base colour   FolkArt™ BaseCoat: Licorice.

Paint   FolkArt™ Acrylic Colors: Harvest Gold, Wicker White, Shamrock, School Bus Yellow, Ultramarine, Cinnamon, Gingersnap, Huckleberry.

Varnish   FolkArt™ Satin Finish Water Base Varnish.

Brushes   No. 5 round, No. 3 round, No. 2 liner.

Other materials   White transfer paper, stylus, materials for antiquing (page 29).

Preparation   Refer to instructions for preparation of metal (page 26). Apply Licorice basecoat, and allow to dry. Apply a thin coat of Satin Finish Water Base Varnish. When dry, transfer the pattern.

Scroll border   Load No. 5 round brush with Harvest Gold, paint the comma strokes, and allow to dry. Load No. 2 liner brush with Wicker White, and paint thin lines over each comma, following the edge of the comma. Use a stylus to make dots of lace in Wicker White.

Large leaves   Load No. 5 round brush with Shamrock, mix with a little School Bus Yellow, and paint the base colour of the large leaves; allow to dry. Load the brush with Shamrock, top-load with Wicker White, and paint comma strokes over the leaves. Use No. 2 liner brush to do fine linework with Wicker White on the leaves.

Small leaves and stems   Load No. 5 round brush with Shamrock, top-load with School Bus Yellow, and paint small leaves. Load No. 2 liner brush with Shamrock and paint fine scrolls, also the fine stems from the flowers.

Commas   Load No. 5 round brush with Shamrock, top-load with Wicker White, and paint commas coming into the central stem.

Large tulip   Load No. 5 round brush with Ultramarine mixed with a little Wicker White, and paint the base colour of the tulip shape; allow to dry. Load the brush with Ultramarine, top-load with Wicker White, and paint over the base colour of the tulip as shown on the colour worksheet page 10.

Small tulips   Load No. 3 round brush with Cinnamon, top-load with Wicker White and paint the petals.

Bluebell flowers   Mix a medium blue from Ultramarine and Wicker White. Load No. 5 round brush with it, top-load with Wicker White, and paint small bells. Load No. 2 liner brush with Wicker White

Pattern for borders and central design

and paint commas from bells.

Poppies Load No. 5 round brush with Gingersnap, top-load with Wicker White, and paint the petals. For the centre, use Huckleberry top-loaded with School Bus Yellow. Make dots with Huckleberry. Refer to the colour worksheet on page 10.

Dot daisies Using the stylus, make Wicker White dots for petals. Make centre dot with School Bus Yellow.

Finish Varnish with Satin Finish Water Base Varnish. Follow the instructions for antiquing (page 29). Finish with a coat of varnish.

Colonial Kettle with Australian Bouquet

(Photograph page 12)

Colonial cooks must have been strong, for kettles like this one are very heavy. My 10 quart (11 litre) kettle was manufactured by T. & C. Clark and Co. Ltd, England, and branded 'First Quality'. Try to find beautiful metal items for your painting, and keep them for future generations.

Base colour   FolkArt™ BaseCoat: Bottle Green.

Paint   FolkArt™ Acrylic Colors: Evergreen, Wicker White, School Bus Yellow, Harvest Gold, Buttercrunch, Plum Pudding, Huckleberry, Paisley Blue, Spanish Tile, Christmas Red, Green Olive, Robin's Egg, Licorice.

Varnish   FolkArt™ Satin Finish Water Base Varnish.

Brushes   No. 2 liner, No. 5 round, No. 3 round.

Other materials   White transfer paper, poly sponge, stylus.

Preparation   Refer to instructions for preparation of metal (page 26). Apply Bottle Green basecoat, and allow to dry. Transfer the pattern. Refer to colour worksheet page 7 for flower details.

Spiky leaves   On the area of each spiky stalk in the pattern, use a poly sponge to dab gently a mixture of Evergreen and Wicker White. Try not to blend the colours on the sponge; they must show as separate small dots in the background. Load No. 2 liner brush with Evergreen, top-load with Wicker White, and paint a thin stem in the centre of each sponged area, from the top to the base of each spiky stalk. Reload the brush, and paint thin leaf strokes coming from the outside into the centre stem; continue down the stem, stroking on each side. Paint a few centre strokes top-loaded with School Bus Yellow.

Gold cluster flowers   Using the wooden end of your brush, load with Harvest Gold and Buttercrunch, and make large and small dots in a circle.

Purple flowers   Load No. 5 round brush with Plum Pudding, top-load with Wicker White, and paint two leaf strokes for each petal. Load the brush with Huckleberry, top-load with School Bus Yellow, and paint the centre in a crescent shape.

Blue flowers   Follow the above instructions but substitute Paisley Blue for the Plum Pudding.

Everlasting daisy   Load No. 2 liner brush with School Bus Yellow, top-load with Wicker White and paint thin 'leaf strokes' coming from the outside of the flower into the centre, all around each daisy; allow to dry. Load No. 2 liner brush with Spanish Tile, top-load with Wicker White, and paint thin strokes over the first petals, casually filling in the daisy. Load

68

No. 5 round brush with Huckleberry, top-load with a little Wicker White and School Bus Yellow, and paint the centre in a crescent shape, joined.

Boronia   Using the wooden end of your brush, make Wicker White dots for petals. Make centre dot with Cherry Royale.

Christmas bells   Load No. 5 round brush with Christmas Red and paint bell shapes using comma strokes. Allow to dry, reload brush with Christmas Red, top-load with School Bus Yellow, and paint comma strokes over the bell shape to form outer flower petals.

Waratah   Using No. 5 round brush, paint Christmas Red base colour. For centre petals, load brush with Christmas Red, top-load with Wicker White and paint comma strokes over base circle. For outer petals, load brush with Christmas Red, top-load with Licorice and paint leaf strokes to form outer petals.

Border and trim   Paint the borders with Green Olive. Make dot daisies with Wicker White petals and School Bus Yellow centre. Paint comma strokes with Buttercrunch.

Flannel flowers   Load No. 5 round brush with Wicker White, top-load with a little of Robin's Egg, and paint the petals as comma strokes coming from the centre of the flower to the outer edge. Load the brush with Robin's Egg, top-load with a little Licorice, and dab in the centre of the flower. Using the stylus, highlight with Wicker White dots in the centre. Load No. 5 round brush with Robin's Egg, top-load with Wicker White, and paint comma strokes for the leaves.

Yellow daisies   Load No. 3 round brush with Harvest Gold, top-load with Wicker White, and paint small crescent shapes, joined. Using the wooden end of your brush, make a centre dot with Cherry Royale.

Finish   Varnish with FolkArt™ Satin Finish Water Base Varnish.

Small Picture Frame

(Photograph page 13)

Picture frames can be decorated in many ways to complement a treasured photograph. For this small frame I have chosen a cottage scene with a daisy trim. The details are shown in the colour worksheet on page 7.

Base colour   FolkArt™ BaseCoat: Butter Pecan.

Paint   FolkArt™ Acrylic Colors: Taffy, Green Meadow, Bayberry, Harvest Gold, Brownie, Glazed Carrots, School Bus Yellow, Wicker White, Calico Red, Nutmeg, Ultramarine.

Varnish   FolkArt™ Satin Finish Water Base Varnish.

Brushes   No. 4 flat, No. 3 round, No. 1 liner.

Other materials   Transfer paper, sponge stick, stylus.

Preparation   Refer to instructions for preparation of wood (page 26). Apply Butter Pecan basecoat with a sponge stick and allow to dry. Transfer the pattern.

Edge of frame   Load No. 4 flat brush with Taffy, and paint trim line around edge of frame. Using the stylus, paint Taffy dots around the edge of trim.

Daisy leaves   Load No. 3 round brush with Green Meadow, top-load with Bayberry, and paint leaf strokes. For small leaves, paint strokes with Harvest Gold. For leaf stems, use No. 1 liner brush and paint with Brownie.

Daisy   Load No. 3 round brush with Glazed Carrots, top-load with Wicker White, and paint the petals as comma strokes coming from the outer edge of each petal into the centre. Load the brush with

Brownie, top-load with School Bus Yellow, and paint the centre. Add dots in Wicker White.

Small pink flowers   Load No. 3 round brush with Calico Red, top-load with Wicker White, and paint the flower tubes. At the top of each flower, make a Wicker White dot.

Tiny daisy   Using the stylus, make Wicker White dots for petals. Make centre dot with School Bus Yellow.

THE COTTAGE   Using No. 4 flat brush, paint the walls and roof with a mixture of Nutmeg and Taffy. Shade edge of walls with Brownie.

Roof   Load No. 4 flat brush with Harvest Gold, then double-load the brush with Taffy, and paint with short flat strokes across the roof (see colour worksheet page 7). Load No. 1 liner brush with Wicker White, and paint fine lines over the roof to show thatching.

Windows   Using No. 3 round brush, paint the window area with Taffy. Outline the windows with Brownie.

Door   Using No. 3 round brush, paint the door with Calico Red. Outline it with Brownie.

Path   Using No. 4 flat brush, side-load with Nutmeg and wash down each side of the path, keeping the loaded side of the brush towards the grass edge.

Bushes   Load No. 3 round brush with Green Meadow, top-load with Wicker White, and dab in the tree and bushes.

Grass   Side-load No. 4 flat brush with Green Meadow, and gently apply as a wash in the areas of grass up to the edge of the path.

Flowers   Using your stylus, dot in some flowers, in Calico Red top-loaded with Wicker White; Ultramarine and Wicker White; and School Bus Yellow and Wicker White.

Finish   Varnish with FolkArt™ Satin Finish Water Base Varnish.

71

Oval Picture Frame

(Photograph page 13)

Sprays of roses, cornflowers and wheat adorn this picture frame, with a background and borders of gentle green.

Base colour   FolkArt™ BaseCoat: Porcelain White.

Paint   FolkArt™ Acrylic Colors: Thicket, Huckleberry, Bayberry, Evergreen, Plantation Green, School Bus Yellow, Ultramarine, Wicker White, Cherry Royale, Taffy.

Varnish   FolkArt™ Satin Finish Water Base Varnish.

Brushes   No. 5 round, No. 6 flat, No. 2 liner.

Other materials   Stylus, transfer paper, sponge stick.

Preparation   Refer to instructions for preparation of wood (page 26). Apply Porcelain White with sponge stick over the whole item and allow to dry.

Borders   Paint the outer edge trim of the frame with Thicket. Then basecoat the entire piece with Bayberry. Using No. 6 flat brush, side-load with Bayberry, and paint a wash around the inner edge of the frame. Using the wooden end of your brush or a large stylus, make a dot trim around inner edge in Evergreen, alternating with Taffy. When dry, transfer the pattern.

Leaves and stems   Load No. 5 round brush with Evergreen, paint the large leaves and allow to dry. Load the brush with Evergreen, top-load with Huckleberry, and make comma strokes over the large leaves. For medium-sized leaves, load the brush with Plantation Green, top-load with Wicker White, and paint leaf strokes. For small leaves, load the brush with Evergreen and top-load with School Bus Yellow. Paint stems with No. 2 liner brush in Huckleberry, top-loaded with Wicker White.

Wheat   Load No. 5 round brush with Huckleberry, top-load with School Bus Yellow, and dab in the grains of wheat, in rows of two, from the base of the flower to the edge of the pattern. Load No. 2 liner brush with Huckleberry, and paint fine lines coming from each grain.

Cornflowers   Load No. 5 round brush with Ultramarine, top-load with Wicker White, and paint small crescent-shaped petals. Make a centre dot in School Bus Yellow, surrounded by dots of Huckleberry.

Roses   Load No. 5 round brush with Cherry Royale, paint the base colour of each rose, and shade the top and lower edges in Huckleberry, and allow to dry. Load the brush with Cherry Royale, top-load with Wicker White, and paint comma strokes to form the petals.

Finish   Varnish with FolkArt™ Satin Finish Water Base Varnish.

Metal Lunch Box

(Photograph page 13)

I don't know the early history of this tin box, but it may have been a miner's lunch box, holding not only the food but also a container of hot tea. It is just the right size for carrying paints and brushes when I travel.

Base colour   FolkArt™ Base Coat: Taffy.
Paint   FolkArt™ Acrylic Colors: Taffy, Huckleberry, Teal Green, Wicker White, Evergreen, School Bus Yellow, Thicket, Calico Red, Metallic Pure Gold, Licorice.
Varnish   FolkArt™ Satin Finish Water Base Varnish.
Brushes   No. 5 round, No. 3 round, No. 2 liner, No. 6 flat brush.
Other materials   FolkArt™ Extender, poly sponge, feather for veins in marble effect, transfer paper, stylus.

Preparation   Refer to instructions for preparation of metal (page 26). Apply a basecoat of Taffy and allow to dry. Then apply a thin coat of Satin Finish Water Base Varnish.
Sponge marbling   Place on your palette a puddle of Taffy and a puddle of Huckleberry, also a few drops of Extender. Load the sponge with Taffy, then a little Extender, then a little Huckleberry; dab the sponge on the palette to remove excess paint. Sponge the entire item. See page 9. Use a feather loaded with Taffy for the veining.

Edging   Load No. 6 flat brush with Taffy and paint the trim. Load the No. 2 liner brush with Huckleberry, and paint the base colour of the cord. Load No. 2 liner brush and paint fine 'S' strokes over the cord in Taffy.
Scrolls   Load No. 3 round brush with Teal Green, top-load with Wicker White, and paint the scrolls.
Leaves   Load No. 5 round brush with Evergreen, top-load with School Bus Yellow, and paint leaf strokes. Load No. 2 liner brush with Thicket, and paint the stems.
White daisies   Load No. 3 round brush with Wicker White, and paint 'leaf strokes' for the petals. Paint the centres with School Bus Yellow. Using a stylus, make dots around centres with Huckleberry.
Roses   Load No. 5 round brush with Calico Red, and paint the base colour of the rose shapes. Shade top and lower edge of roses with Huckleberry, and allow to dry. Load No. 5 round brush with Calico Red, top-load with Wicker White, and paint comma strokes to form the petals. Make Wicker White dots in centres.
Filler commas   Paint with Thicket top-loaded with Wicker White, using No. 3 round brush.
Latches   Metallic Pure Gold.
Handle   Licorice.
Finish   Varnish with FolkArt™ Satin Finish Water Base Varnish.

Pattern for sloping top and side panels

Pattern for end panels

Rose-covered Jewellery Box

(Photograph page 13)

Sponged marbling is a pretty background for the roses framed in gold on this wooden box. I painted the jewellery box during a workshop with my students.

Base colour   FolkArt™ Base Coat: Taffy.

Paint   FolkArt™ Acrylic Colors: Taffy, Cherry Royale, Honeycomb, Shamrock, Chocolate Fudge, Olive Green, Wicker White, Metallic Pure Gold.

Varnish   FolkArt™ Satin Finish Water Base Varnish.

Brushes   No. 8 flat, No. 6 flat, No. 2 liner, No. 3 round.

Other materials   FolkArt™ Extender, poly sponge, transfer paper.

Preparation   Refer to instructions for preparation of wood (page 26). Paint the box with Taffy, and allow to dry. Apply a thin coat of Satin Finish Water Base Varnish.

Sponged marbling   Place on your palette separate puddles of Cherry Royale, Taffy and Honeycomb, plus a few drops of Extender. Gently dab the sponge in Taffy, then a little Extender, then Honeycomb, and gently press it on your palette to remove excess paint; sponge the entire box. Wash and dry the sponge, then load it with a little Extender and Cherry Royale; gently sponge just a hint of colour on the box, and allow to dry. Apply a thin coat of Satin Finish Water Base Varnish. When dry, transfer the pattern.

Leaves   Load No. 8 flat brush with Shamrock, side-load with Chocolate Fudge, and paint the leaves. Outline with Green Olive using No. 2 liner brush. Load No. 3 round brush with Green Olive, and paint the smaller leaves.

Roses   Load No. 6 flat brush with Cherry Royale, side-load with Wicker White, and paint using the Flat Brush Rose Technique as shown in the colour worksheet page 8.

Gold trim on box edge   Paint with Metallic Pure Gold using No. 6 flat brush..

Bow   Load No. 3 round brush with Cherry Royale, top-load with Wicker White, and paint the bow.

Finish   Varnish with FolkArt™ Satin Finish Water Base Varnish.

Pattern for top of box

Bow and ribbon trim for around side of box

Tulip–Garland Parlour Clock

(Photograph page 13)

The soft blended finish of the flat brush techniques used by decorative artists, inspired me to design this delicate clockface. The technique of blending with a flat brush takes a little practice, but it is worth persevering.

Base colour FolkArt™ BaseCoat: Porcelain White.

Paint FolkArt™ Acrylic Colors: Taffy, Rose Garden, Evergreen, Thicket, Wicker White, Seafoam, Brownie, Cotton Candy, School Bus Yellow, Blueberry Pie, Harvest Gold, Metallic Pure Gold, Licorice.

Varnish FolkArt™ Satin Finish Water Base Varnish.

Brushes No. 6 flat, No. 4 flat, No. 2 liner, No. 3 round.

Other materials Sponge for marbling, transfer paper, stylus.

Preparation Apply Porcelain White basecoat.

Marble background Place on your palette separate puddles of Taffy and Rose Garden. Using a damp small sponge, dab gently in Taffy, then in Rose Garden, and pat the sponge on the palette until just a small amount of the two colours emerges from the sponge. Gently dab the sponge over the whole background of the clockface. If the colours become spotty, moisten the sponge with a little water, and blend the colours; it must be a very delicate show of colours, blending against the background colour. Allow to dry. Seal with a thin coat of Satin Finish Water Base Varnish. Transfer the pattern.

Leaves Load No. 6 flat brush with Evergreen, paint the base area of all leaves, and allow to dry. Double-load the brush with Thicket and Wicker White, and paint the detail of each leaf.

Ribbon Load the No. 6 flat brush with Seafoam, and paint the ribbon; allow to dry. Double-load the brush with Evergreen and Wicker White, and paint over the Seafoam ribbon, placing highlights in the centre of the ribbon.

Tulips Paint base area of tulip shapes with Rose Garden using No. 6 flat brush. Shade with Brownie. Highlight with Cotton Candy. In the centre of open flowers, use a stylus to make dots with Wicker White, School Bus Yellow and Brownie.

Blue flowers Double-load No. 4 flat brush with Blueberry Pie and Wicker White, and paint flower tubes. Using a stylus, make a Wicker White dot at the tip of each flower. Load No. 2 liner brush with Brownie, and paint fine stems from the petals.

Yellow flowers As for blue flowers, but substitute Harvest Gold for Blueberry Pie.

Clock dial Side-load No. 6 flat brush

with Wicker White, and wash over the central area. Use the stylus to make the dot trim with Wicker White.

Numbers   Load No. 3 round brush with Metallic Pure Gold and paint the numbers. Outline numbers with Licorice.

Border   Load No. 3 Round Brush with Metallic Pure Gold and paint a border of commas. Using a stylus, make Harvest Gold dots around the border.

Finish   Varnish with FolkArt™ Satin Finish Water Base Varnish.

Breakfast Tray

(Photograph page 13)

Having grown up with the soft colours of England, I designed this tray using the colours I remember from childhood. The flat brush technique of blending colours gives a realistic effect especially to flowers.

Base colour   FolkArt™ Base Coat: Milkshake.

Paint   FolkArt™ Acrylic Colors: Metallic Pure Gold, Shamrock, Bayberry, Huckleberry, Apricot Cream, Wicker White, School Bus Yellow, Calico Red, Plum Pudding, Honeycomb, Paisley Blue.

Varnish   FolkArt™ Satin Finish Water Base Varnish.

Brushes   No. 8 flat, No. 6 flat, No. 4 flat, No. 5 round, No. 2 liner.

Other materials   Transfer paper, FolkArt™ Extender, poly sponge.

Preparation   Refer to instructions for preparation of wood (page 26). Apply a basecoat of Milkshake, and allow to dry. Trim with Metallic Pure Gold. When dry, apply a thin coat of Satin Finish Water Base Varnish. Transfer the pattern.

Leaves   Load No. 8 flat brush with a little Extender; this will give you extra time for blending your colours. Now load the brush with Shamrock, side-load with Bayberry, and paint the leaves using the flat brush technique shown on the colour worksheet on page 6. Side-load No. 6 flat brush with Huckleberry, and shade the edge of larger leaves. Load No. 2 liner brush with

Huckleberry, and paint the stems.

Apricot carnations   Load No. 6 flat brush with Apricot Cream, side-load with a little Huckleberry, then on the other side of the brush side-load with Wicker White; blend colour across the brush on your palette. Paint three rows of petals, starting with the longer outer row and working into the centre of the flower. Paint the centre with School Bus Yellow; shade with Huckleberry; and highlight with Wicker White.

Rosebuds   Paint the base area with Calico Red using No. 4 flat brush. Load No. 5 round brush with Shamrock, top-load with Bayberry and a little Huckleberry, and paint comma strokes to form the greenish sepals.

Rose   Refer to the colour worksheet on page 8 for details of the flat brush technique. Use No. 8 flat brush, with Calico Red, Huckleberry for shading and Wicker White.

Purple daisies   Load No. 8 flat brush with Plum Pudding, side-load with Wicker White, and paint crescent strokes for the petals. In the centre, paint a base of School Bus Yellow; shade with Huckleberry and Wicker White; and dot with School Bus Yellow and Wicker White.

Tan daisies   As for purple daisies, but substitute Honeycomb for Plum Pudding.

Blue daisies   Load No. 8 flat brush, with Paisley Blue, and paint a base shape for each flower. Load the brush with Paisley Blue, side-load with Wicker White, and paint the inner petals, keeping the highlight in the centre of the petal. Load No. 2 liner brush with Huckleberry, and paint fine lines from the flower's centre over the petals. Load No. 5 round brush with School Bus Yellow, and paint a base colour in the centre; shade with Huckleberry, and highlight with Wicker White.

Filler flowers   Using No. 4 flat brush, make crescent strokes for each little flower, with Apricot Cream, Wicker White, Calico Red and Plum Pudding.

Filler commas   Metallic Pure Gold applied with No. 5 round brush.

Finish   Varnish with Satin Finish Water Base Varnish.

Timber Welcome Sign

(Photograph page 14)

Most of us have a 'Dream Cottage'. Somewhere quiet, away from the clamour of the city, surrounded by beautiful flowers and trees. This sign belongs to mine. Every time I hang a coat on the hook it's a welcoming feeling.

Wood staining   FolkArt™ Acrylic Color: Nutmeg. Refer to the directions for wood staining (page 26).

Paint   FolkArt™ Acrylic Colors: Shamrock, Huckleberry, Wicker White, Christmas Red, School Bus Yellow, Taffy, Paisley Blue, Chocolate Fudge.

Varnish   FolkArt™ Satin Finish Water Base Varnish.

Brushes   No. 4 round, No. 6 flat, No. 2 liner, stipple or deerfoot brush.

Other materials   Poly sponge for wood staining, chalk or transfer paper.

Preparation   Apply a thin coat of Satin Finish Water Base Varnish over the stained timber piece. Side-load No. 6 flat brush with Shamrock, and wash the background area where the house will be painted, using horizontal flat strokes. When the green paint is dry, draw the pattern freehand or by transfer paper.

Lettering   Load No. 4 round brush with Huckleberry, and paint the lettering. When dry, shade with Wicker White.

Tulips   Load the No. 4 round brush with Christmas Red, top-load with Wicker White and School Bus Yellow, and paint the petals.

Leaves   Load the brush with Shamrock, top-load with Taffy, and paint the leaves.

White daisy   Paint the petals with Wicker White. Shade near the centre with Chocolate Fudge. Dab in centre with School Bus Yellow.

Scrolls   Using No. 2 liner brush, paint scrolls with Chocolate Fudge.

House   Mix a caramel colour from Huckleberry and Taffy with a little School Bus Yellow. Using No. 6 flat brush, paint the walls caramel. When dry, shade with Chocolate Fudge. Paint the door Huckleberry with a little School Bus Yellow; outline with Chocolate Fudge. Paint the windows Taffy; outline with Chocolate Fudge. For roof, paint alternate rows of Huckleberry mixed with School Bus Yellow, Chocolate Fudge, and Taffy. With No. 2 liner brush, paint thin lines over the roof area in Chocolate Fudge, and Wicker White, to define thatching.

Bushes   Using a stipple or deerfoot brush, load with three colours: Shamrock, School Bus Yellow, Wicker White. Test the colours have not blended on the brush, because the three colours are to show separately. Dab or pat in the shrubs on the left-hand side of the house, and also the climbing plants where they reach the roof. Stipple a darker green mix of shrubs on the right-hand side of the house.

Tree   Load No. 4 round brush with Huckleberry, top-load with Wicker Whiteand Chocolate Fudge, and paint the tree trunk. Using a stipple brush or deerfoot brush, load with three colours: Shamrock, Wicker White, School Bus Yellow. Stipple in the foliage of the tree.

Path   Side-load No. 6 flat brush with Shamrock, and wash the side edges of the path to define it.

Flowers   Using No. 4 round brush, stipple different coloured flowers around the cottage with Paisley Blue, Christmas Red, Wicker White, School Bus Yellow.

Finish   Varnish with FolkArt™ Satin Finish Water Base Varnish.

Pattern for trim repeated either side of "Welcome"

Timber Coat Rack

(Photograph page 14)

Hooks for coats and hats and other things always seem to be useful in our house. In this coat rack the soft apricot colour of the poppies seems to tone well with the stained timber and a classical green border.

Wood staining   FolkArt™ Acrylic Color: Nutmeg. Refer to the directions for wood staining (page 26).

Paint   FolkArt™ Acrylic Colors: Evergreen, School Bus Yellow, Mystic Green, Wicker White, Brownie, Spanish Tile, Calico Red, Ultramarine, Buttercrunch.

Varnish   FolkArt™ Satin Finish Water Base Varnish.

Brushes   No. 5 round, No. 2 liner, No. 6 flat.

Other materials   Poly sponge for wood staining, transfer paper, stylus.

Preparation   Apply a thin coat of Satin Finish Water Base Varnish over the stained timber piece. Transfer the pattern, allowing for the border trim.

Leaves   Load No. 5 round brush with Evergreen, paint the base area of the three large leaves, and allow to dry. Reload the brush with Evergreen, top-load with School Bus Yellow, and paint comma strokes over the base colour. Load No. 5 round brush with Mystic Green, top-load with Wicker White, and paint the smaller leaves. Load No. 2 liner brush with Brownie, and outline each leaf with 'S' strokes.

Poppies   Load No. 5 round brush with Spanish Tile, paint the base area of each poppy, and allow to dry. Load No. 5 round brush with Wicker White, and place thick dabs of paint along the top edge of the flower; do not rinse the brush; roll it on the palette to remove excess paint, then load it with Spanish Tile, and make comma strokes pulling the white paint towards the centre of the flower. Continue this process for each petal. (Refer to the colour worksheet page 10 for details.) For the centre of the open poppy, load No. 2 liner brush with Calico Red, and paint thin lines coming from the centre to the outside of the petal. Load No. 5 round brush with Brownie, top-load with School Bus Yellow, and dab in the centre of the poppy. Using a stylus, make Wicker White dots.

White flowers   Load No. 5 round brush with Wicker White, and paint 'leaf strokes' for the petals. Load No. 2 liner brush with Brownie, and paint fine lines coming from the centre of the flower. Load No. 5 round brush with School Bus Yellow, and dab in the centre. Using the stylus or the wooden end of your brush, make Brownie dots around the yellow centre. Make Wicker White dots at the tip of each petal.

Blue flowers   Load No. 5 round brush with Ultramarine, top-load with Wicker White, and paint tiny crescent shapes for the petals. Using the wooden end of your brush, make a Brownie dot in the centre.

Surround it with dots of School Bus Yellow.

Border trim   Use a No. 6 flat brush to paint in Evergreen and use No. 2 liner brush for 'S' shape and dot trim in Buttercrunch.

Finish   Varnish with FolkArt™ Satin Finish Water Base Varnish.

Wooden Spoon Holder

(Photograph page 14)

My husband, Dieter, made this wooden spoon holder for our kitchen when my collection of spoons grew too large for the drawer. The fruit design can be adapted for use on other items, too.

Wood staining   FolkArt™ Acrylic Color: Pecan Pie. Refer to the directions for wood staining (page 26).

Paint   FolkArt™ Acrylic Colors: Seafoam, Evergreen, School Bus Yellow, Brownie, Christmas Red, Wicker White, Harvest Gold, Plum Pudding, Licorice, Thicket.

Varnish   FolkArt™ Satin Finish Water Base Varnish.

Brushes   No. 5 round, No. 6 flat, No. 2 liner.

Other materials   Poly sponge for wood staining, transfer paper, stylus.

Preparation   Apply a thin coat of Satin Finish Water Base Varnish over the stained timber piece. Transfer the patterns for the front and side panels.

Leaves   Load No. 5 round brush with Seafoam, paint the base area of all large leaves, and allow to dry. Load No. 5 round brush with Evergreen, top-load with School Bus Yellow, and paint the detail of the grape leaves and apple leaves. Load the brush with Evergreen, top-load with Brownie, and paint over the pear leaves.

Apple   Paint the base colour for the apple with Christmas Red using No. 5 round brush. Side-load No. 6 flat brush with Brownie, and shade the left-hand side of the apple. Rinse brush, side-load with Wicker White, and highlight the right-hand side of the apple. See colour worksheet page 7.

Pear   Paint the base colour for the pear with Harvest Gold using No. 5 round brush. Side-load No. 6 flat brush with Brownie, and shade the left-hand side of the pear. Rinse brush, side-load with Wicker White, and highlight the right-hand side of the pear.

Grapes   Paint the base colour for the grapes with Plum Pudding using No. 5 round brush. Using No. 6 flat brush, shade individual grapes with Licorice; and highlight them with Wicker White. Load No. 2 liner brush with Thicket, and paint thin curly lines as shown on the pattern.

Strawberries   Paint the base colour for each strawberry with Christmas Red using No. 5 round brush. Load No. 6 flat brush with Brownie, and shade left-hand side of each strawberry. Rinse brush, load with School Bus Yellow, and highlight the right-hand side. Using the stylus, make Licorice dots for seeds; over each one, dot with School Bus Yellow, then a little Wicker White. Load No. 5 round brush with Evergreen, top-load with Wicker White, and paint green leaves on top of each strawberry. Paint the strawberry flowers using No. 5 round brush with Wicker White for petals, a centre dot of

Evergreen, and a smaller dot of School Bus Yellow.

Scroll border Load No. 5 round brush with Harvest Gold, top-load with Wicker White, and paint a series of commas.

Add Wicker White dots.

Trim On top and side of the box, paint Christmas Red, using No. 6 flat brush.

Finish Varnish with FolkArt™ Satin Finish Water Base Varnish.

Front panel design

Base panel design

Side panel design

Stained Timber Stool

(Photograph page 15)

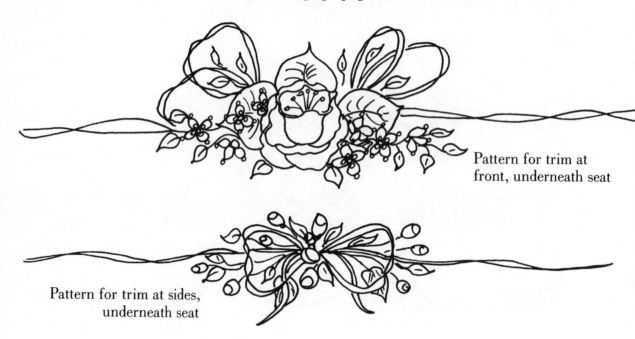

Pattern for trim at
front, underneath seat

Pattern for trim at sides,
underneath seat

Traditional folk artists decorated their furniture with scenes that were most familiar to them, perhaps a village setting enhanced by a floral border. Here I have painted our family pet, Daisy, in the European Alps because she reminds me of alpine cows.

Wood staining   Refer to the directions for oil-based wood stains (page 28).

Paint   FolkArt™ Acrylic Colors: Ultramarine, Wicker White, Huckleberry, Chocolate Fudge, School Bus Yellow, Licorice, Bayberry, Buttercrunch, Taffy, Shamrock, Blue Gray Dust, Calico Red.

Varnish   FolkArt™ Satin Finish Water Base Varnish.

Brushes   No. 6 flat, No. 4 flat, No. 2 liner, No. 5 round, No. 3 round.

Other materials   Transfer paper, stylus.

Preparation   Apply a thin coat of Satin Finish Water Base Varnish over the stained timber piece. Transfer the pattern. It will be necessary to transfer the pattern again over the background paint when dry.

SCENE   Mix a medium blue from Ultramarine and Wicker White, load No. 6 flat brush with it, and paint the sky.

Alps   Load the brush with Huckleberry, side-load with Chocolate Fudge, and paint the mountains, keeping the dark side of the brush at the top. Allow to dry, then side-load the brush with Wicker White, and paint snow on the mountains.

Pattern for seat of stool

Corner trim for Stained Timber Stool

Hills   Load the brush with School Bus Yellow, side-load with a little Licorice, and paint the hills.
Foreground   Load the brush with Bayberry, side-load with a little Chocolate Fudge, and wash in the grassed areas.

Road   Load the brush with Buttercrunch, and paint the base of the road. Shade with Huckleberry.
Buildings   Using No. 4 flat brush, paint the walls with Buttercrunch. Shade with Huckleberry. Load No. 6 flat brush with

Huckleberry, side-load with Chocolate Fudge, and paint the roof areas. Using No. 2 liner brush, paint the windows with Taffy. Outline them with Chocolate Fudge.

Pine trees   Load No. 5 round brush with Shamrock, top-load with Bayberry and Wicker White, and paint 'leaf strokes' coming from the trunk to the outer edge of the tree.

Cow   Load No. 3 round brush with Licorice, and paint the cow. Highlight with Wicker White.

Fence   Load No. 2 liner brush with Blue Gray Dust, top-load with Wicker White, and paint the fence.

FLORAL BORDER   Load No. 6 flat brush with Shamrock, side-load with Bayberry, and paint the leaves. Load No. 2 liner brush with Shamrock, and paint veins on leaves.

Ribbon   Mix a pale blue from Ultramarine and Wicker White. Load No. 3 round brush with it, and paint the ribbon and bows.

Yellow rosebuds   Load No. 4 flat brush with School Bus Yellow, side-load with Wicker White, and paint small rosebuds coming from the bow.

White flowers   Side-load No. 6 flat brush with Wicker White, and paint the petals. Using a stylus make centre dot with School Bus Yellow.

Rose   Load No. 6 flat brush with Calico Red, side-load with Wicker White, and paint with the flat brush technique. Using No. 2 liner brush, make fine lines for centre stamens with Wicker White and dots at the end. (Refer to the colour worksheet page 8.)

Finish   Varnish with FolkArt™ Satin Finish Water Base Varnish.

Painter's Case

(Photograph page 15)

This is my very first painting case, so it holds great memories for me. It is now decorated with a Bavarian scene from the area where my husband grew up and where we have spent wonderful times together.

Base colour   FolkArt™ BaseCoat: Robin's Egg.

Paint   FolkArt™ Acrylic Colors: Ultramarine, Wicker White, Chocolate Fudge, Licorice, Evergreen, School Bus Yellow, Bayberry, Poppy Seed, Skintone, Huckleberry, Wintergreen, Thicket, Calico Red, Taffy.

Varnish   FolkArt™ Satin Finish Water Base Varnish.

Brushes   No. 8 flat, No. 6 flat, No. 4 flat, No. 2 liner, No. 3 round, No. 5 round.

Other materials   Tracing paper (dark), stylus, poly sponge.

Preparation   Refer to instructions for preparation of wood (page 26). Apply basecoat of Robin's Egg, and allow to dry. Apply a thin coat of Satin Finish Water Base Varnish. Transfer the pattern.

BAVARIAN SCENE   Mix a medium blue from Ultramarine and Wicker White, load No. 8 flat brush and paint the sky. Side-load No. 6 flat brush with Wicker White, and paint the clouds.

Alps   Load No. 8 flat brush with Chocolate Fudge, side-load with Licorice, and paint the mountains, keeping the dark side of the brush at the top. Allow to dry.

Side-load the brush with Wicker White, and wash in the snow on the mountains.

Hills   Load No. 8 flat brush with Evergreen, side-load with a little School Bus Yellow, and paint the hills.

Road   Load No. 8 flat brush with a mixture of School Bus Yellow and a little Chocolate Fudge, and paint the road. When dry, side-load No. 6 flat brush with Chocolate Fudge, and shade each side of the road.

Foreground grass   Load No. 8 flat brush with Bayberry, and paint the grass. Side-load the brush with Chocolate Fudge, and shade in small ridges in the grass. When background paint is dry, re-transfer the pattern onto the background. Side-load No. 8 flat brush with Poppy Seed, and shade along the ridge where the village sits, then along the edge of the road, and in the meadow to form small rises. Load No. 2 liner brush with Huckleberry, and paint the fences. Load the brush with Licorice and paint the small cows.

Village   Load No. 3 round brush with Wicker White, and paint the buildings, paint the roofs with Chocolate Fudge top-loaded with a little School Bus Yellow.

Trees at village   Load No. 5 round brush with Poppy Seed, top-load with Evergreen and School Bus Yellow, and dab in the trees and bushes around the buildings.

House   Mix a clay colour from Huckleberry, Wicker White, and School

91

Front panel of Painter's Case

Back panel of Painter's Case

Bus Yellow, and paint walls using No. 6 flat brush. Side-load the brush with Huckleberry, and shade the edges of the walls. Load No. 5 round brush with Chocolate Fudge, top-load with Wicker White, and paint the door in straight strokes. For windows, mix a soft cream from Wicker White and a little School Bus Yellow, outline in Chocolate Fudge (refer to the colour worksheet page 7 for detail).

Tables and stools   Load No. 3 round brush with Chocolate Fudge, top-load with Wicker White, and paint tables and stools. For beer glasses, School Bus Yellow highlighted with Wicker White.

Large trees   For foliage, sponge a mix of Wintergreen, Bayberry and School Bus Yellow. Use No. 3 round brush to paint the apples Calico Red and Wicker White. Paint the trunks Chocolate Fudge and Wicker White.

Dancing girl   Load No. 3 round brush with Calico Red, and paint the dress. Paint blouse with Wicker White. Side-load No. 4 flat brush with Huckleberry, and shade in the skirt. Side-load No. 4 flat brush with Wicker White, and wash in the apron. Load No. 3 round brush with School Bus Yellow, top-load with Wicker White and paint the hair. Using a stylus, make dots of Calico Red, Ultramarine and Wicker White to form the flowers in the hair. Face: base coat with Skintone or mix a small amount of Huckleberry and Wicker White; paint details using No. 2 liner brush with Huckleberry. Stockings: paint in Wicker White using No. 3 round brush. Shoes: paint in Licorice using No. 3 round brush.

Dancing boy   Load No. 4 flat brush with Poppy Seed and paint the jacket. When dry, side-load the brush with Licorice, and shade the edge of the jacket. Paint the pants Wintergreen; shade with Licorice. Paint the shirt Wicker White. Face: follow

instructions for the Dancing girl. Hair: using No. 3 round brush, mix a dark brown from Huckleberry and a small amount of Licorice, top-load with Wicker White. Stockings: using No. 3 round brush, basecoat in Wicker White. Side-load No. 4 flat brush with Licorice and shade detail.

Man at the table   Use No. 3 round brush. Jacket: paint with Thicket, highlight with Wicker White. Hair: Huckleberry top-loaded with Wicker White. Features: Skintone or mix a small amount of Huckleberry and Wicker White; paint details using Huckleberry on No. 2 liner brush.

Floral garland   Using your stylus, dot in separate dots of Calico Red, Ultramarine and Evergreen to form flowers in the garland. For the ribbons, use Calico Red and Ultramarine on No. 2 liner brush top-loaded with Wicker White.

FLORAL BORDER   Frame the scene with a border painted in Wintergreen, using No. 8 flat brush.

Leaves   Load No. 5 round brush with Poppy Seed, paint base area of leaf shapes, and allow to dry. Load No. 5 round brush with Evergreen, top-load with School Bus Yellow, and paint comma strokes over the leaves. For smaller leaves, load the brush with Poppy Seed top-loaded with Wicker White.

Comma fillers   Load No. 3 round brush with Evergreen and paint the comma fillers.

Roses   Load No. 5 round brush with Calico Red, and paint the base colour of the rose shape. Load the brush with Calico Red, top-load with Wicker White, and paint over each rose with comma strokes to form the petals, as shown on the colour worksheet on page 10.

Blue flowers   Load the wooden end of your brush with Ultramarine, dip into Wicker White, and make dots for the petals. Make centre dot with School Bus Yellow.

White daisies   Load No. 3 round brush with Wicker White, and paint in 'leaf strokes' for the petals. Load the brush with Huckleberry, top-load with School Bus Yellow, and dab in the centre.

Finish   Varnish with FolkArt™ Satin Finish Water Base Varnish.

BACK PANEL   Load No. 8 flat brush with Taffy and paint base colour under floral bouquet. Frame this area with a border painted in Wintergreen, using No. 8 flat brush.

Bouquet

Leaves   Load No. 5 round brush with Poppy Seed, paint base area of leaf shapes and allow to dry. Load No. 5 brush with Evergreen, top-load with School Bus Yellow and paint comma strokes over the leaves. For smaller leaves, load brush with Poppy Seed top-loaded with Wicker White.

Roses   Load No. 5 round brush with Christmas Red and paint base colour of rose shape, top-load with Wicker White and paint over each rose with comma strokes to form the petals.

Ribbon   Load No. 5 round brush with a medium blue mixed from Ultramarine and Wicker White, top-load the brush with Wicker White and paint in the bow.

Small white flowers   Load the wooden end of your brush with Wicker White and make dots for the petals. Make centre dots with School Bus Yellow. Make smaller single dots on pattern in Ultramarine and Wicker White.

Floral border

Paint the floral border around the bouquet in the same manner. Load No. 3 round brush with Evergreen and paint the comma fillers.

White daisies   Load No. 3 round brush with Wicker White and paint in leaf strokes for the petals. Load the brush with Huckleberry, top-load with School Bus Yellow, and dab in the centres.

Blue flowers   Load the wooden end of your brush with Ultramarine, dip into Wicker White and make dots for the petals. Make centre dots with School Bus Yellow.

Border on edge of case   Load No. 2 liner brush with Calico Red and paint thin leaf shape. Dot in Wintergreen and dot between in Calico Red.

Finish   Varnish with FolkArt™ Satin Finish Water Base Varnish.

Wooden Box with Bavarian Couple

(Photograph page 15)

Traditional folk artists commemorated special events by painting timber boxes and furniture. A popular item was the wedding box, in which a couple would store mementoes of the day. On this small round box I have painted a couple in traditional Bavarian dress.

Base colours   FolkArt™ BaseCoat: Antique Red, Indigo.

Paint   FolkArt™ Acrylic Colors: Calico Red, Blueberry Pie, Wicker White, Harvest Gold, Skintone, Pecan Pie, Buttercup, Licorice, Huckleberry, Fresh Foliage, Green Olive, Evergreen, School Bus Yellow, Holiday Red.

Varnish   FolkArt™ Satin Finish Water Base Varnish.

Brushes   No. 6 flat, No. 4 flat, No. 1 liner, No. 3 round, No. 5 round.

Other materials   White transfer paper, stylus, sponge stick.

Preparation   Refer to instructions for preparation of wood (page 26). Apply Antique Red basecoat with sponge stick over entire box, and allow to dry. Paint a circular area on the top of the box with Indigo. When dry, transfer the pattern. Refer to colour worksheet page 9.

The woman   Using No. 6 flat brush, paint the skirt Calico Red, apron Blueberry Pie, vest Calico Red, blouse Wicker White, scarf Harvest Gold, face and hands Skintone, stockings Wicker White, shoes Pecan Pie, hair Buttercup, basket Harvest Gold. Two coats of paint may be necessary for a good coverage. Then shade the skirt, shoes and vest with Licorice. Shade the apron and blouse with a dark grey mixed from Licorice and a little Wicker White. Shade the face and arms with Huckleberry, using No. 4 flat and No. 1 liner brushes. For the hair, load No. 3 round brush with Pecan Pie, top-load with a little Huckleberry, and paint small curly comma strokes over base colour.

The man   Using No. 6 flat brush, paint the shirt Wicker White, jacket Fresh Foliage, pants Pecan Pie, hat Green Olive mixed with a little Licorice, socks Wicker White, shoes Pecan Pie, face and knees Skintone, hair Pecan Pie. Shade the jacket with Evergreen, pants Huckleberry, socks Green Olive, shoes Licorice, hat Licorice, shirt a light grey mixed from Licorice and a little Wicker White. Paint the facial details with Huckleberry, using No. 4 flat and No. 1 liner brushes. For the hair, load No. 3 round brush with Pecan Pie, top-load with a little Licorice, and paint comma strokes over base colour.

Flowers in basket   Load No. 3 round brush with Evergreen, top-load with School Bus Yellow, and paint the leaves. To make roses with dots, dip the wooden end of the brush into Calico Red and then into Wicker White, and dot the flowers over the leaves.

FLORAL BORDER   Load No. 5 round brush with Evergreen, and paint the leaves. Load the brush with Green Olive, top-load with Wicker White, and make comma strokes on leaves. Load the brush with Harvest Gold, top-load with Wicker White, and paint the filler commas.

Daisy   Paint comma strokes with Wicker White, alternating thick commas and thin. For the centre, paint Huckleberry top-loaded with School Bus Yellow. Highlight the centre with Wicker White dots.

Blue flower   Load No. 5 round brush with Blueberry Pie, top-load with Wicker White, and paint comma strokes pulling

Repeat floral pattern around central lid panel and box sides

Trim for edge of box lid

from the centre of the flower to the outside. For the centre, paint Huckleberry top-loaded with School Bus Yellow. Highlight the centre with Wicker White dots. Make fine-line detail on petals with Huckleberry using No. 1 liner brush.

Red flower   Paint a basecoat for all petals with Calico Red using No. 5 round brush. Load No. 5 round brush with Holiday Red, top-load with Wicker White, and paint 'leaf strokes' into the centre. For the centre, paint Huckleberry top-loaded with School Bus Yellow. Highlight the centre with Wicker White dots.

Border trim   Harvest Gold, Blueberry Pie, School Bus Yellow using No. 1 liner brush.

Finish   Varnish with FolkArt™ Satin Finish Water Base Varnish.

Wooden Clogs

(Photograph page 15)

At last, I have painted my daughter's clogs. The design is styled on traditional Dutch painting known as *Hindeloopen*. The Hindeloopers were originally known for their fine carving of small wooden items. Then they began to imitate and paint the designs of their carvings onto larger pieces of furniture, and soon developed this unique style.

Base colour FolkArt™ BaseCoat: Antique Red.

Paint FolkArt™ Acrylic Colors: Ultramarine, Tapioca, Evergreen, Brownie, Buttercup, Chocolate Fudge, Calico Red, School Bus Yellow, Wicker White, Licorice, Mystic Green, Seafoam, Spanish Tile.

Varnish FolkArt™ Satin Finish Water Base Varnish.

Brushes No. 3 round, No. 1 liner, No. 2 liner, No. 4 flat, No. 6 flat.

Other materials White transfer paper, stylus, chalk.

Preparation Refer to instructions for preparation of wood (page 26). Apply Antique Red basecoat and allow to dry. Two coats may be necessary. Transfer the patterns: each clog has its own scenic panel.

Scene Mix a soft blue from Ultramarine and Tapioca, load No. 6 flat brush, and paint the sky. Mix a similar blue for the river.

Grass Load the brush with Evergreen, and paint the banks on either side of the river. Re-transfer the pattern, especially the house, boat, trees, etc.

House Load No. 4 flat brush with Brownie, lightened by adding a little Tapioca, and paint the walls and roof area. When the base colour of the roof is dry, load No. 3 round brush with Brownie, top-load with Tapioca, and pull down strokes from the top of the roof line to the top of the walls. Paint the windows with Buttercup. Using No. 1 liner brush, outline the windows with Chocolate Fudge. Side-load No. 4 flat brush with Brownie, and shade the walls of the house. Load No. 3 round brush with Calico Red, and paint the door. Using No. 1 liner brush, outline the door with Chocolate Fudge.

Trees and bushes Load No. 3 round brush with Evergreen, top-load with a little School Bus Yellow and Wicker White, and dab in the trees and bushes along the edge of the river. Load No. 1 liner brush with Brownie, and paint the tree trunks.

Clouds Side-load No. 4 flat brush with Wicker White, and wash in the clouds.

Boat in the river Load No. 3 round brush with Chocolate Fudge, top-load with Wicker White, and paint the boat.

Fisherman Using No. 3 round brush, paint the pants with Calico Red, the shirt Wicker White, the hat Licorice.

Birds Load No. 1 liner brush with

Trim for open edges of clogs

Pattern for back
of clogs

Pattern for top right clog

Toe trim for clogs

Pattern for top left clog

Licorice, and paint bird shapes.

Repeat the process to paint the scene on the other clog.

FLORAL BORDER   Note that two coats of the base colour for flowers and leaves may be necessary on the dark background.

Leaves   Load No. 3 round brush with Mystic Green, and paint the base colour of all leaf shapes. Using No. 1 liner brush with Tapioca, overstroke the leaves.

Blue tulips   Load No. 3 round brush with Seafoam, and paint tulip shapes. Shade the tulips with Brownie in small 'S' strokes. Highlight with Wicker White in small 'S' strokes. This technique is done with a round brush and is called unblended shading.

Yellow tulips   As for blue tulips, but substitute Buttercup for Seafoam.

Open roses   Load No. 3 round brush with Spanish Tile, and make a doughnut shape for each rose. Change to No. 6 flat brush, side-load with Brownie, and shade right-hand side of the circle. Load the brush with Wicker White, and on the left-hand side highlight the outer edge. Using sharpened chalk, redraw the petal shapes over the base colour once dry. Load No. 2 liner brush with Wicker White, paint small comma strokes for the outer edge of the petals, and make fine lines in each petal. For the centre, use No. 3 round brush to apply School Bus Yellow. When dry, use No. 4 flat brush to shade with Brownie and highlight with Wicker White. Using the stylus, make Wicker White dots that gradually become smaller around the centre.

Scroll border   Load No. 2 liner brush with Tapioca, and paint comma border as shown on the pattern.

Finish   Varnish with FolkArt™ Satin Finish Water Base Varnish.

Seaman's Uniform Trunk

(Photograph page 12)

This old trunk was manufactured by John Burton 'Box and Chest Maker', Falcon Factory, Lower Whitecross Street, London E.C., according to the label attached to the inside of the trunk. Metal trunks like this were meant to last, and with a new coat of paint they will serve a few more generations.

Base colours　FolkArt™ BaseCoat: Licorice, Porcelain White.

Paint　FolkArt™ Acrylic Colors: Shamrock, Huckleberry, Wicker White, School Bus Yellow, Licorice, Buttercup, Seafoam, Honeycomb, Buttercrunch, Mystic Green, Cherry Royale.

Varnish　FolkArt™ Satin Finish Water Base Varnish.

Brushes　No. 8 flat, No. 6 round, No. 2 liner, stipple or deerfoot brush.

Other materials　Transfer paper, poly sponge.

Preparation　Refer to instructions for preparation of metal (page 26). Apply Licorice basecoat, and allow to dry. On areas of design, apply Porcelain White basecoat, and allow to dry.

SHIP SCENE　Transfer only some areas of the pattern: cliff, foreshore and ocean. For the sky, using No. 8 flat brush, wash a little Shamrock over the Porcelain White background.

Cliffs　Load No. 8 flat brush with Shamrock, side-load with Huckleberry, and paint the cliffs. Highlight with Wicker White.

Foreshore　Load No. 8 flat brush with Shamrock, side-load with School Bus Yellow, and paint the foreshore.

Rocks and beach　Load No. 6 round brush with Huckleberry, top-load with a little Licorice, and dab in the rocks. Highlight with Wicker White. Load No. 6 round brush with Buttercup, top-load with Wicker White, and dab in the beach.

Ocean　Load No. 8 flat brush with Shamrock, and apply a base colour over the ocean area; load brush with Seafoam, side-load with Wicker White, and paint ridges to form waves.

Ship　Transfer ship pattern. Refer to the colour worksheet page 9 for detail. Paint the hull's base area with Honeycomb using No. 6 round brush; shade with Huckleberry. Paint the sails' base area with Wicker White; shade with a soft grey mixed from Wicker White and a little Licorice.

Trees and shrubs　Load a stipple or deerfoot brush with Shamrock, top-load with School Bus Yellow, and dab in the foliage of trees and shrubs.

Rope border　Paint the base area of the border with Buttercrunch using No. 8 flat brush, and allow to dry. Load No. 8 flat brush with Buttercrunch, double-load with Huckleberry, and paint 'S' strokes over the base colour, reloading after every second

Pattern for top panel of Seaman's Uniform Trunk

Trim for edge of trunk lid

Pattern for side panel of trunk

Pattern for end panel of trunk

stroke. Load No. 2 liner brush with Wicker White, and paint small 'S' strokes over the rope to highlight it.

FLORAL BORDER AND PANELS Transfer the pattern for the floral border on the top of the trunk.

Leaves Load No. 6 round brush with Shamrock, top-load with Mystic Green and a little Wicker White, and paint the leaves.

Scroll border Load No. 6 round brush with Buttercup, top-load with Wicker White, and paint the scrolls.

Daisies Load No. 6 round brush with Wicker White, and paint comma strokes for the petals. Load the brush with Huckleberry, top-load with School Bus Yellow, and dab in the daisy centre. Load No. 2 liner brush with Honeycomb, top-load with Wicker White, and paint the stems.

Roses Load No. 6 round brush with Cherry Royale, and paint base area of the rose shape; allow to dry. Load the brush with Cherry Royale, top-load with Wicker White, and paint comma strokes for the petals. Refer to the colour worksheet on page 10 for detail.

Side and end panels Follow the instructions given above for painting the floral panels with rope and scroll borders.

Finish Varnish the whole trunk with FolkArt™ Satin Finish Water Base Varnish.

Cow Bell

(Photograph page 15)

When snow lies deep on the ground and the cows are safe in the barn, there's time for the folk artist–farmer to decorate old cow bells such as these.

Base colour   FolkArt™ BaseCoat: Rusty Nail.

Paint   FolkArt™ Acrylic Colors: Rusty Nail, Ultramarine, Wicker White, Huckleberry, School Bus Yellow, Licorice, Calico Red.

Varnish   FolkArt™ Satin Finish Water Base Varnish.

Brushes   No. 6 flat, No. 4 round, No. 2 liner.

Other materials   White transfer paper.

Preparation   Refer to instructions for preparation of metal (page 26). Apply a basecoat of Rusty Nail over the bell. Trace the pattern, adjusting it to the size of the bell.

Sky   Mix a soft blue colour from Ultramarine and Wicker White, and using No. 6 flat brush paint the sky with horizontal flat strokes.

Snow-covered land   Load the No. 6 flat brush with Wicker White, and paint the entire ground area with horizontal flat strokes. When dry, side-load the brush with Huckleberry, and wash in the top of the hills and ridges to define them.

It will be necessary to transfer the details of the pattern once again onto the background paint when dry.

Background trees   Mix a dark green from Ultramarine and School Bus Yellow and a little Wicker White. Load No. 4 round brush with it, top-load with Wicker White, and gently dab along the back ridges to give a hint of trees.

Church   Mix a soft cream from School Bus Yellow, Huckleberry and Wicker White. Load No. 4 round brush with it, and paint the walls. Mix a grey from Licorice and Wicker White for the roof. Paint the door Calico Red.

Barn   Paint the front wall Licorice top-loaded with Huckleberry, the roof Wicker White, the door Huckleberry, using No. 4 round brush.

House   Mix Calico Red, Huckleberry and a little Wicker White, and paint the front and side walls. Mix School Bus Yellow and Wicker White, and paint the windows. Mix Licorice and Wicker White, and paint the roof. Outline the windows and door in Licorice. Paint the door Calico Red.

Foreground trees   Load the No. 4 round brush with Huckleberry and just a tip of Wicker White, and paint the trunks and branches only.

Icy stream   Paint a soft wash of grey mixed from Licorice and Wicker White.

Alpine flower border   Mix a soft green from Ultramarine, School Bus Yellow and Wicker White. Load the No. 4 round brush with it, top-load with School Bus Yellow, and paint all the leaves. Using

No. 2 liner brush, load with Huckleberry
and top-load with Wicker White and paint
the stems. For Edelweiss, paint Wicker
White petals, and centre dot in School Bus
Yellow. For Alpenrose buds, Calico Red,
top-loaded with Wicker White. For blue
daisies a mixture of Ultramarine and
Wicker White.

Comma borders Mix a soft cream
colour from School Bus Yellow and Wicker
White, load the No. 4 round brush with it,
then top-load with Wicker White, and
paint a series of commas.

Reverse side Paint the Alpenrose with
Calico Red, top-loaded with Wicker White.
Paint the leaves green mixed from
Ultramarine, School Bus Yellow and
Wicker White. Paint the ribbon pale blue
mixed from Ultramarine and Wicker
White.

Finish Apply three coats of Satin Finish
Water Base Varnish.

Trim for back
of bell

Pattern for
front of bell

Pattern for
side of bell

Trim for top of bell handle

Antiqued Bavarian Wall Clock

(Photograph page 15)

My inspiration for this clockface was an old museum piece with a similar shape. The floral border is painted with very casual and relaxed brushstrokes, perhaps as it would have been painted a century ago.

Base colour   FolkArt™ BaseCoat: Chocolate Fudge.

Paint   FolkArt™ Acrylic Colors: Chocolate Fudge, Ultramarine, Wicker White, Shamrock, School Bus Yellow, Buttercrunch, Calico Red, Licorice, Metallic Pure Gold.

Varnish   FolkArt™ Satin Finish Water Base Varnish.

Brushes   No. 5 round, No. 2 liner, No. 6 flat.

Other materials   White transfer paper, stylus, materials for antiquing (page 29), sponge stick.

Preparation   Refer to instructions for preparation of wood (page 26). Apply a basecoat of Chocolate Fudge, and allow to dry. Apply a thin coat of Satin Finish Water Base Varnish. Transfer the pattern and use a compass to draw the clock dial.

SCENE   Using No. 6 flat brush, paint in the background starting at the top. For the sky, use Ultramarine mixed with Wicker White for a light blue. The mountains Chocolate Fudge, washed with Wicker White for snow. The hill and foreground, Shamrock mixed with a little School Bus Yellow. Transfer the pattern once again onto the background paint when dry.

House   Using No. 5 round brush, paint the walls Buttercrunch mixed with a little Chocolate Fudge. The roof Calico Red. The windows pale blue mixed from Ultramarine and Wicker White. The door Chocolate Fudge. The detail Chocolate Fudge.

Trees   Shamrock top-loaded with Wicker White using No. 5 round brush.

Bushes   Shamrock top-loaded with School Bus Yellow and Wicker White.

Boy   Pants in Shamrock. Coat in Calico Red.

Girl   Dress in Calico Red. Blouse and apron Wicker White.

FLORAL BORDER AND DIAL

Leaves   Shamrock top-loaded with a little School Bus Yellow and Wicker White using No. 2 liner brush.

Roses   Calico Red, Licorice, Wicker White.

Tulips   Ultramarine, Wicker White.

Dot daisies   Wicker White.

Numbers   Wicker White, highlighted with Metallic Pure Gold.

Leaves on the dial   Shamrock top-loaded with School Bus Yellow.

Finish   Apply a thin coat of Satin Finish Water Base Varnish. When dry, follow the instructions for antiquing on page 29. Finish with two coats of Satin Finish Water Base Varnish.

Our House Sign

(Photograph page 16)

Many years ago I designed this timber sign. My husband cut the pieces (he now has a jig saw, which is a useful piece of equipment in a folk artist's home), and I painted a rose-covered cottage with more detail than the other cottages in this book. The profusion of leaves in the garden was created by sponging.

Wood staining   FolkArt™ Acrylic Color: Nutmeg. Refer to the directions for wood staining (page 28).

Paint   FolkArt™ Acrylic Colors: Evergreen, Thicket, Wicker White, Bayberry, Huckleberry, Ultramarine, Honeycomb, Calico Red, Nutmeg, Licorice, Plum Pudding.

Varnish   FolkArt™ Satin Finish Water Base Varnish.

Brushes   No. 5 round, No. 3 round, No. 2 liner, No. 6 flat.

Other materials   Poly sponge, stylus.

Preparation   Refer to the instructions for preparation of wood (page 26). Transfer the pattern.

TOP SECTION

Leaves   Load No. 5 round brush with Evergreen, top-load with Thicket, and paint comma strokes for large leaves coming from base of the rose to their outer edge. Top-load with Wicker White, and paint a highlight stroke on the edge of each leaf. For small leaves, load No. 5 round brush with Evergreen, top-load with Bayberry, and paint leaf strokes.

Yellow flower spikes   Load No. 3 round brush with School Bus Yellow, top-load with Wicker White, and dab colour along the stems.

Blue tulips   Load No. 5 round brush with Ultramarine, top-load with Wicker White, and paint 'leaf strokes' to form a tulip (refer to colour worksheet page 10 for detail).

Comma fillers   Load No. 3 round brush with Honeycomb, top-load with Wicker White, and paint comma strokes.

Rose   Load No. 5 round brush with Calico Red, and paint the base colour of the rose shape; allow to dry. Load the brush with Calico Red, top-load with Wicker White, and paint over the rose with comma strokes to form the petals. (Refer to colour worksheet page 10 for detail.)

Lettering   Use No. 2 liner brush, and paint with Thicket. Highlight with Honeycomb, top-loaded with Wicker White.

COTTAGE   Load No. 6 flat brush with Honeycomb, paint walls and roof of the house, and allow to dry.

Roof   Load No. 6 flat brush with Nutmeg, double-load with Honeycomb, and paint rows across the roof. Reload if paint becomes blended. Load the brush with Honeycomb, double-load with Wicker

White, and paint every second row to resemble thatching. Use No. 2 liner brush to define with Wicker White.

Windows   Load No. 5 round brush with Honeycomb, and paint the windows. Use No. 2 liner brush to outline with Huckleberry.

Door   Load No. 5 round brush with School Bus Yellow, top-load in Licorice, and paint long strokes for the door. Outline with Huckleberry.

Garden foliage   Load the poly sponge with Evergreen, Bayberry and Thicket, and sponge in the foliage of the garden, including the climbing plants.

Red flowers   Load No. 3 round brush with Calico Red, top-load with Wicker White, and dab in roses over the front door, and hollyhocks under the window.

Lilac-coloured flowers   Load No. 3 round brush with Plum Pudding, top-load with Wicker White, and dab in the flowers climbing up to the roof. Paint other flowers in the garden with Calico Red, School Bus Yellow, Ultramarine and Wicker White, using the above method.

Border   Paint dark edge in Thicket using No. 6 flat brush.

Finish   Varnish with FolkArt™ Satin Finish Water Base Varnish.

Index

A
acryl-blend, 21–22
acrylic painting, 32
alphabet, 18
antiquing, 29
Australian bouquet, *12*, 68–69
B
Bauernmalerei rose, *8*
Bavarian couple, *9, 15*, 96–97
Bavarian scene, *9*
belt buckles, *1*, 34, 35
Biedermeier style, 20
bisque porcelain preparation, 27
border trims, *8, 9, 10*
boronia, 7
bracelets *1*, 38, 39–40
brooches, *1*, 36, 37
brushes, 21, 32
brushstrokes, *6, 10*, 23–25
C
'C' or crescent shape brushstrokes, *6*, 24
candle and soap preparation, 27
ceramic duck, *3*, 41–42
ceramic pots, *2*, 46–47
clay preparation, 27
colour, 31–32
colour worksheets, *6–10*
comma strokes, *6, 8*, 23
cottage, 7
creamer, *2*, 48–49
creating patterns, 31
cross-hatching, *6*
D
daisies, *6, 8*, 38, 41, 43, 60
dots, graduating, *6*
double side-loading, 24–25

E
equipment, 21–22
eraser, 22
everlasting daisy, 7
extender, 21–22
F
fabric preparation, 27
fine lines, 25
flannel flower, 7
flat brush rose, *8*
flat brushes, loading, 24
flat brushstrokes, *6*
flower details, 7
foreshore, *9*
freehand sketching, 31
fruit details, 7
G
glass preparation, 27
glazed surface preparation, 27
H
Hindeloopen flower, *8*
history of folk art, 20
hue, 32
I
intensity (colour), 32
L
lace border, *8*
leaf shape, *6*, 23–24
left-side comma, 23
loading a flat brush, 24
loading a round brush, 23
loading a second colour, 24
loading a single colour, 23, 24
M
materials, 21–22
medium, 21–22

metal preparation, 26–27
metal projects
   coal-scuttle, *12*, 66–67
   colonial kettle, *12*, 68–69
   cow bell, *15*, 104–05
   creamer, *2*, 48–49
   dairy bucket, *12*, 64–65
   lunch box, *13*, 74–75
   parlour heater, *11*, 62–63
   trunk, *12*, 101–03
mixing colours, 31–32
mountain scene, 7

P

painting hints, 30–32
paints, 21
palettes, 22
paper preparation, 27
patterns, 30–31
picture frames, *13*, 70–71, 72–73
poly sponge, 22
poppies, *10*, 36, 43, 67
porcelain preparation, 27
preparation of surfaces, 26–27

R

retarder, 21–22
ribbon strokes, 6
right-side comma, 23
rope trim, 9
roses, *8*, *10*, 34, 37, 43, 62, 64, 103
round brushes, loading, 23, 24
round brushstrokes, 6

S

'S' shape brushstrokes, 24
sandpaper, 22
scene details, 7
scene painting, 32
script liner brush, 25
scroll border, *10*
scrolls, 25
sealer, 22
shading, 25
ship, 9
side-loading a flat brush, 24
single-loading a flat brush, 24
sponge marbling, 9, 34, 74, 76, 78
sponge stick, 22
staining, 28–29

stylus, 22
surface, preparation, 26–27

T

tack cloth, 22
temperature (colour), 32
terracotta pots, *2*, 46–47
terracotta preparation, 27
timber *see* wood
top-loading a round brush, 6, 24
transfer paper, 22, 30
transferring patterns, 30–31
tulips, *10*, 60, 66, 78

V

value (colour), 32
varnish, 22

W

waratah flower, 7
washes, 25
water jar, 22
wet palette, 22
white chalk, 22
wood preparation, 26
wood projects
   Austrian plate, *11*, 53–55
   Bavarian wall clock, *15*, 106–07
   bell, counter, *11*, 51–52
   box, oval, *3*, 43–45
   box with Bavarian couple, *15*, 96–97
   bracelets, *1*, 38, 39–40
   breakfast tray, *13*, 80–81
   brooches, *1*, 36, 37
   buckles, *1*, 34, 35
   clogs, *15*, 98–100
   coat rack, *14*, 84–85
   egg, *11*, 56–57
   house sign, *16*, 108–09
   jar, *11*, 50
   jewellery box, *13*, 76–77
   key holder, *11*, 58–59
   painter's case, *15*, 91–95
   pan, *11*, 60–61
   parlour clock, *13*, 78–79
   picture frames, *13*, 70–71, 72–73
   spoon holder, *14*, 86–87
   stool, *15*, 88–90
   welcome sign, *14*, 82–83
wood staining and antiquing, 28–29

Acknowledgments

Special thanks to my husband, Dieter, for his great support and
constructive criticism;
To my children, and especially the youngest, Louise, who had to make her
own breakfast for many mornings;
To all my students, who have taught me many things and supported me
over the years;
To Alison Snepp, for her help and confidence in me;
To Myart Australia, for supplying the paint and materials used in this book;
To Patricia Herd and Fay Bourke, who cared for the busy studio;
To Pauline Dunsire, who helped me in the early years;
To Kirsty Melville, who gave me the opportunity to write this book, and also
Julia Cain and Karen Williams from Simon & Schuster Australia.

TRADITIONAL FOLK ART

First published in Australasia in 1992 by
Simon & Schuster Australia
20 Barcoo Street, East Roseville NSW 2069

Reprinted 1992, 1993, 1994

A Paramount Communications Company
Sydney New York London Toronto Tokyo Singapore

© Janet Klepatzki, 1992

Published by Blitz Editions
an imprint of
Bookmart Limited
Registered Number 2372865
Trading as Bookmart Limited
Desford Road
Enderby
Leicester
LE9 5AD

Designed by Christie & Eckermann Art and Design Studio
Photographs by Jonathan Chester/Extreme Images
Typeset in Australia by Asset Typesetting Pty Ltd
Printed in Hong Kong by South China Printing Company